"Hi' Racing Brother Dale"
Ed Iskenderian 2019

607

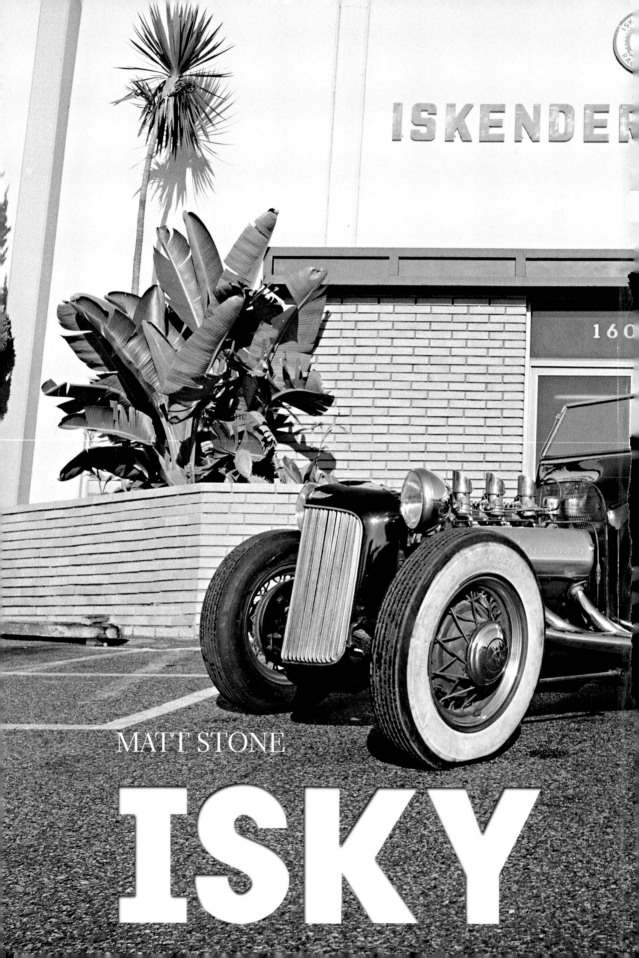

MATT STONE

ISKY

ED ISKENDERIAN AND
THE HISTORY OF
HOT RODDING

CarTech ®

CarTech®, Inc.
838 Lake Street South
Forest Lake, MN 55025
Phone: 651-277-1200 or 800-551-4754
Fax: 651-277-1203
www.cartechbooks.com

Edit by Bob Wilson
Design Concept by Connie DeFlorin
Layout by Monica Seiberlich

ISBN 978-1-61325-290-1
Item No. CT570

Library of Congress Cataloging-in-Publication Data Available

Written, edited, and designed in the U.S.A.
Printed in China
10 9 8 7 6 5 4 3 2

Front Cover: "Hiya Pal – can I help ya?" Walk into the lobby hallway at Isky Racing Cams, and it is possible that a warm and always smiling Camfather will greet you. Isky understands the Internet's many innovations and benefits, but still enjoys print as a medium, and it remains an important element in his company's ongoing advertising and marketing efforts. The first advertisement he ran after going into business was in Hot Rod in the late 1940s, and he still supports many hot rod, muscle car, and racing magazines. (Photo Courtesy MelStonephoto.com)

Front Flap: The much talked about, elegant, and artistic hand-cast radiator mascot that Isky bought from a friend for $2. He recalls that a half dozen or so of them were made at the time, something any hot rodder would be proud to bolt to his car, then or today.

Endpapers: Isky and his famous roadster in front of his Inglewood, California, shop. Notice that the car looks particularly fresh here, with gleaming, polished valvecovers, intake stacks, and exhaust, with shiny black paint on the charming Model T "turtle deck" bodywork. (Photo Courtesy Ed Iskenderian)

Frontispiece: This compelling photograph is as much pure unadulterated Isky as any I've ever seen. He's out in the shop, barking an order or telling a story, requisite cigar blazing away. (Photo Courtesy Holly Martin)

Title Page: Ed never failed to get a shot of his legendary hot rod in front of each of his new shops. This is the current Gardena, California, location when it opened in the mid-1960s. (Photo Courtesy TEN: The Enthusiast Network)

Contents Page: Here, Isky shows off an early homemade version of a valvetrain dynamometer. This machine only mounts the valvetrain of one cylinder to make the measurement, then the power draw of this test is multiplied by the number of cylinders in the subject engine to determine the overall number. (Photo Courtesy Mel Stone)

Back Cover Photos

Top: Even though Ed's roadster sat a fair bit as his family and business grew, he wasn't shy about taking it to the streets and blowing out the cobwebs every once in a while. The date and location aren't known for sure, but it's likely somewhere in Inglewood or Culver City, California, near Ed's shop in the late 1950s or early 1960s. The width of the street and the prevalence of new construction are clues. (Photo Courtesy TEN: The Enthusiast Network Archive)

Bottom: Isky leads the way out to the Spintron shop and his personal outdoor treasure chest. Ed's cruiser beanie hat is omnipresent; occasional bouts of poor circulation sometimes leave his hands a little cold, so he'll often wear gloves around the shop. (Photo Courtesy Mel Stone)

DISTRIBUTION BY

Europe
PGUK
63 Hatton Garden
London EC1N 8LE, England
Phone: 020 7061 1980 • Fax: 020 7242 3725
www.pguk.co.uk

Australia
Renniks Publications Ltd.
3/37-39 Green Street
Banksmeadow, NSW 2109, Australia
Phone: 2 9695 7055 • Fax: 2 9695 7355
www.renniks.com

Contents

DEDICATION

It is with great honor and consideration that I dedicate this book to my late mother, Bella, and my late father, Milt, both of whom would be 91 if they were still with us; to 94-year-old Ed Iskenderian; and his lifelong friend, 95-year-old John Athan.

They were all children of the 1920s, born of immigrant parents, who survived the Great Depression, World War II and other wars, raised families, and built often-great businesses without the benefit of rich parents or "formal" higher education. They understood the meaning of hard work, the principles of ethics, and the need for honesty and integrity. They each had the drive to create, innovate, and love, and have served the country that gave them the freedom and opportunities to live meaningful lives.

These notable people are part of the reason their era is called the Greatest Generation.

ACKNOWLEDGMENTS AND THANKS . . .

First and foremost, to Mr. Isky himself, for unselfishly sharing with me many hours of his time and his story so this book could happen. At the tender age of 95, Ed is one of the most amazing men I've ever known.

My thanks also go to the rest of the Isky Racing Cams gang, for their generous support for anything I needed, most particularly Ed's sons, Richard, Ron, and Timothy Iskenderian. And, Nick Arias, John Athan, Robert "Bones" Balough, Mel Carlisle, Bob Collum, Monika Earle, Vic Edelbrock Jr., Kirk Gerbracht, Sidney Hidalgo, Kurt Hooker, Maria Jones, Robert Jung, Ed Justice Jr., Dave McClelland, Tom Madigan, Steve Magnante, Holly Martin, Paul Pfaff, Wayne Phillips, Greg Sharp, Bob Steinhagen, Linda Stone, the NHRA Museum, and Tom Voehringer.

Finally, my thanks to you for reaching into your (real or metaphorical) wallet to buy this book. For without you, there would be no reason or opportunity to do this. I hope you enjoy this great story.

Publisher's Note: In reporting history, the images required to tell the tale will vary greatly in quality, especially by modern photographic standards. While some images in this volume are not up to those digital standards, we have included them, as we feel they are an important element in telling the story.

FOREWORD

This is a young, tall, handsome Vic Edelbrock Jr. cranking away on an overhead valve V-8 engine, either assembling, uncrating, or preparing it for a dynamometer test. Even though Edelbrock is among the deans of the high-performance parts production industry, he still knows his way around an engine and spent plenty of time as a young man getting his hands dirty at his father's shop, before it became his in the early 1960s. (Photo Courtesy Edelbrock LLC)

Vic Edelbrock Sr. and Jr. are leaning on a stack of what the company initially built its name and reputation on; cast aluminum intake manifolds. The company catalog now numbers hundreds of pages with thousands of individual parts numbers. (Photo Courtesy Edelbrock LLC)

by Vic Edelbrock Jr.

*V*ic Edelbrock Jr. grew up in the performance business. He's also largely responsible for the high-performance aftermarket industry growing up. His father, Vic Sr., launched the business in the 1930s, and Jr. was ready to take the reins when his father passed away unexpectedly of cancer in late 1962. Vic the younger continued his father's vision of producing innovative and high-quality performance products, which, under his leadership, has expanded far beyond the original product lines initiated by his father. The original business centered on a race shop and engine building. In addition to intake manifolds, valvecovers, heads, carburetors, and such, the company also produces a several-hundred-page catalog filled with other engine components, as well as entire engines; all of the core performance products are "made in the U. S. of A.," as Vic likes to say. Edelbrock is or has been an OEM-level component supplier to all of America's major carmakers, a huge supporter of the Specialty Equipment Market Association (SEMA), and a member of a variety of racing organizations and countless halls of fame. He's also known Ed Iskenderian since they were both young men, and I'm honored that Vic agreed to speak up and out about his old friend "Isky" for this volume.

I first got to know Ed while I was kicking around my dad's (Vic Edelbrock Sr.) shop when I was a kid. I remember when Ed had his little shop on West Adams, then at Slauson and Jefferson, never far from my dad's business, and at one time, just across the street from it. I think Ed had just a couple of employees at the time and only one or maybe two cam-grinding machines. Even though newer overhead valve V-8 engines were coming out of Detroit every year through the 1950s, the Ford flathead V-8

Vic Sr.'s original business was a high-quality but otherwise conventional service and repair station. But it wasn't long before Vic Sr., a fast and capable midget car racer, developed an entire performance business to include race preparation, engine building, and high-performance components manufacture. Edelbrock's facilities were, and remain, first-class properties. (Photo Courtesy Edelbrock LLC)

Ed Iskenderian always remembers Vic Edelbrock Sr. as tall, dark, handsome, and always smiling. The stack of hardware on which he is leaning are Edelbrock high-performance aluminum heads for Ford flathead V-8 engines. (Photo Courtesy Edelbrock LLC)

was still the mainstream viable racing engine for a while throughout the 1930s and 1940s.

We built them for street hot rods, for dry lakes cars, and for midget racing, all things my father was highly involved in personally. My dad had an idea for a camshaft design with a peculiar lobe shape, so he took it to the outfit that, at the time, was considered the leader in the performance camshaft game and asked them to grind him up a cam with this configuration so he could test it. The guys over there took one look at it and said, "This won't work!" and sent him packing. They wouldn't even make him up one to test.

So my dad said, "Forget them," and went to talk it over with Isky. There were some unusual aspects to this design that required some special machining features, but Isky said he could make it. And he did. He gave us the cam, Dad stuck it into an engine, horsepower was way up, and it ran great. So my father took it back over to Ed and said, "You need to produce this." And that led to Ed's famous 404 flathead

Two early greats of hot rod high-performance development, Bobby Meeks (left) and Ed Iskenderian, meet over a hot flathead on the Edelbrock/Isky dynamometer. Meeks was a legendary engine builder, particularly good at hand matching and balancing engine components. (Photo Courtesy Edelbrock LLC)

cam, which became the standard bearer for anyone building a hot flathead.

And Dad ran this cam in his own car, although by this time (1941), a lot of people said the flathead's days were over and that my dad really needed to be running a Chevrolet inline-6, which he absolutely wasn't going to do in his Ford roadster. And, in mid-November 1941, just three weeks before Pearl Harbor, he proved everybody wrong by running his roadster through the traps at 121.4 mph at a Roadrunners club timing meet. Pretty fast for a '32 roadster running a naturally aspirated engine and no special aerodynamic bodywork.

My next memory of Ed was when I was at USC, working for my dad during the summer of 1955. My dad got three of the new small-block Chevy V-8 engines from Ray Brock at *Hot Rod* magazine; these were to be used as R & D engines for the development of racing and high-performance pieces, dyno testing, and so forth. My dad sent a notice out to about 10 different cam grinders, Ed included, inviting them in on the opportunity to develop a high-performance cam for the new Chevy V-8 and submit it for dyno testing. The criteria were fairly simple: the experimental cam had to help the engine put out solidly increased horsepower and let the engine run 6,000 rpm.

In short, everyone but Ed's cam failed in one aspect or another. Some put out more power but couldn't run over 5,500

revs, while only one revved higher but didn't put out any more power, that being Ed Winfield's design; his cam had little tiny lobes on it that didn't move the valves all that much, but I swear it would have run 10,000 if it could have made more power. Isky's cam did both.

Ed had developed a great cam for a guy named Bigelow, who was running a 6-cylinder Chevy with good results. Ed took that cam's design and lobe profiles, and adapted them to the small-block Chevy. Simple idea, but it sure ran. This led to Ed's famous Iskenderian E-2 and E-4 cams, and thus he was able to be one of the first guys to market with cams for the new Chevy V-8, a bit of a coup in those days. They were primarily competition or aggressive street cams and sold gangbusters for Ed. I still run such a cam in one of my boats.

Most of Ed's early shops were pretty humble little places, but when he built his facility on Inglewood Avenue in the late 1950s, it was a real first-class place, with nice offices and a great shop. By then Ed was a real businessman running a serious operation. I remember when he began taking full-page ads in *Hot Rod*. It was so impressive, because that kind of move really demonstrated the growing power of the automotive aftermarket, and it was a big investment step for what was essentially still a relatively small business.

I always crack up when I think about Ed and his daily drivers. He always liked

big Cadillacs or the occasional Lincoln. Remember those are big cars and should seat four or five people, but Ed always filled them up with Coke bottles, books, magazines, fishing gear, catalogs, cams, and miscellaneous car parts, so after a while there's no more room for anyone but Ed; the driver's seat is the only empty seat in these big old cars. But that's just Ed.

March 2016 marked my 57th wedding anniversary to my wife, Nancy, and before we were married, I was riding a Match-less 2-cylinder motorcycle. And I decided that in order to buy an engagement ring,

"Hiya, Pal. Can I help ya?" Walk into the lobby hallway at Isky Racing Cams, and it is pos-sible a warm and always smiling Camfather will great you. With the advent of the Inter-net, the old-fashioned auto parts store catalog rack (left) might someday become a thing of the past. Isky understands the Internet's many innovations and benefits but still enjoys print as a medium, and it remains an important element in his company's ongoing adver-tising and marketing efforts. The first advertisement he ran after hanging his modest shingle and going into business was in Hot Rod magazine in the late 1940s, and he still supports many hot rod, muscle car, and racing magazines. (Photo Courtesy Mel Stone)

I needed to sell the bike. So guess who bought it: of course it was Ed. I don't know how much he really wanted the bike or not, but I think it was his way of "loaning" me the money without it looking like a loan or a gift. He gave me $500 cash for the bike so I could buy Nancy's engagement ring, but I'm not sure he rode it much. When he bought it, I delivered it to him at his shop, and we just rolled it into his office, and it sat there for a long time. One day I guess he finally decided to take it out

to ride and smashed it into a curb; that was about the end of Ed's motorcycling days.

If you know anything about Ed, you know he never throws anything away.

Ed Iskenderian's original friendship with the late Vic Edelbrock Sr. flowed naturally into a long-standing friendship and business relationship with his son, Vic Edelbrock Jr., at left. Vic's a big guy, but this also demonstrates what a compact, barrel-chested man Isky is, shown here with a tie tied (typically) a little bit too short, an Isky Racing Cams hat, and his ever-present stogie. (Photo Courtesy Ed Iskenderian)

This is Edelbrock's current product catalog. (Photo Courtesy Edelbrock LLC)

As an Isky Racing Cams dealer, the Edelbrock Equipment Company sold more than its share of cams for Ed's young business back in the day. (Photo Courtesy Edelbrock LLC)

Along the way, the Edelbrock family sold Vic Sr.'s original '32 roadster; for years this had been his everyday car, his street rod, and his race car. At some point, Vic Jr. came in contact with the family who bought the car and let them know that if it ever came up for sale, he'd like first crack at the deal, given the family connection and history attached to it.

Call it good luck or karma, but the gent who owned it put a note in his wallet instructing his wife to please contact Vic Edelbrock Jr. about the car when the time came to sell it. The late owner's family was nice enough to do so, and even though the price was anything but concessionary, the Edelbrock family was able to reacquire the car. It was restored down to the last nut, grommet, and washer just the way that Vic Sr. built it.

It's very stealthy in all-black lacquer with little chrome or other ornamentation, and built and finished to show quality. In 2007, Ford put together a list, and subsequent show, of the 75 most significant '32 Ford hot rods in celebration of this seminal model's 75th birthday. Vic's car made the list handily and on the first vote.

It is seen here, at that show, held at the Pomona Fairgrounds, site of many great Los Angeles roadster shows, the NHRA Winternationals drag racing meet, and home to the Wally Parks NHRA Racing Museum.

Just look at his office or the backseat of his car. You can call him a hoarder or a packrat, but he came from a generation that didn't waste anything because you never knew when you might need whatever it was. After my dad passed away, I was out in the shop replacing an old parts washer that had a hole in the tank, and it wasn't worth fixing. Ed dropped by just to visit and asked what I was doing with the old washer. I told him I was going to junk it and he said, "Oh no, you can't do that. I'll take it." So he did, and it's probably still sitting out behind Ed's shop, never used or repaired, still with a hole in the tank.

He always looks his customer in the eye, and says, "Hiya, Pal. Now, how can I help you?" because he knows his stuff works and he wants to make sure that person got their money's worth with everything installed right and running properly.

There's only one Ed Iskenderian, and we're damn lucky we have him in our business and our lives.

Vic Edelbrock Jr.

INTRODUCTION

ED ISKENDERIAN'S FIRST HOT ROD
This T-body car was a real eye-stopper when Isky built it in the early days of Hot Rodding in 1938-39 . . . and he still has it to this day!

Best wishes from one Hot Rodder to another
Ed Iskenderian

Long before NASCAR and other racing teams developed the "hero card" giveaway, which fans collect or might even use to snag an autograph from their favorite racing driver, Ed Iskenderian employed the idea to good effect with this 8 x 10 glossy. It was shot many years ago in front of Isky Racing Cams' building at 607 Inglewood Avenue in Los Angeles and shows a younger, dark-haired Isky with his famous Model T–bodied roadster hot rod. If you wrote to Isky and asked for an autograph or a product catalog, you received one of these (for only 25 cents) with your return package. (Photo Courtesy Ed Iskenderian)

As I write this, Ed Iskenderian is preparing to celebrate his 94th birthday, which is today. How does a legend and pioneer of the automotive aftermarket performance parts industry (in this case the production of engine camshafts and valvetrain components) celebrate turning 94? Simple: by enjoying birthday cake and a party with his lifelong friend, John Athan . . . who turns 95 only a few days later.

If you picked up this book, you likely know that Ed Iskenderian's "ISKY" Racing Cams has been an innovator and leader in the performance aftermarket for nearly 70 years. The man they now call Mr. Isky is still at the helm of the company that bears his name, and even pushing 100, still goes to work nearly every day. In the beginning, he was the sole employee of his little camshaft production company,

ED ISKENDERIAN RACING CAMS

THE WORLD'S LARGEST FACILITY FOR DESIGN, TEST AND PRODUCTION OF

RACING CAMS

16020 So. Broadway, Gardena, Calif. 90248
Tel (213) 770-0930

Ever the keen promoter, Isky wanted racers, enthusiasts, and kids alike to have Isky Racing Cams stickers on their car, and he developed many attractive logos and graphics for these highly sought-after stickers. Certainly among the most fun and interesting sprang from when someone dubbed him "The Camfather" during The Godfather movies era. Friend and advertising rep Pete Millar developed the Warner Brothers-esque graphic, complete with Ed's trademark cigar; the likeness is startling. Isky would "grind you a camshaft you could not refuse." (Photo Courtesy Ed Iskenderian)

Isky is ever present at hot rod shows, races, rod runs, and all sorts of automotive events; the line for his autograph is always long. Here Isky and the author visit at the 2015 Gas-serFest II car show at the Automobile Driving Museum in El Segundo, California. (Photo Courtesy Kirk Gerbracht)

with a single cam-grinding machine sitting (on a dirt floor) in the back of friend John Athan's tool-and-die shop in Culver City, California.

Through innovation, consistent hard work, strong ethics, keen promotion, advertising, and what we now call "brand building," Iskenderian built a huge world-wide performance parts business that changed the face of the speed parts game and is still in it.

At the age of 95, you might expect a frail, hard-of-hearing little old man, and that is so *not* Isky. He's not a tall gent, but still sturdy and barrel-chested with clear eyes, a strong rich voice, a firm hand-shake, and an ever-present cigar. Over time, some of racing's very best and most notable drivers have run Isky cams in their cars, particularly in the earliest days of NASCAR, and throughout the post–World War II history of drag and land speed record racing. Of Turkish Armenian descent, he's an American-born citizen, a father and grandfather, and he served his country during World War II in the United States Army Air Corps. He learned machin-ing and life skills in junior high, high school, and the military that helped him launch his own business in his mid-20s, without a college education. Regardless, he's smart, savvy, highly ethical, profes-sional, courteous, well read, and well spo-ken to this day. His memory is better than that of my computer.

He's also a model of consistent solidity: He built a famous Ford hot rod in the 1930s and 1940s and still owns it. He's owned his business and worked essentially the same job for seven decades now, although his sons have taken over much of the day-to-day at Isky Racing Cams. Ed can still grind a camshaft and still owns the machine on which he pro-duced his first one. He eats lunch at the same little South Los Angeles burger joint every day. And he's known his best friend for 87 years.

As I've assembled this book, I've gotten to know this gentle giant of the per-formance industry; we've had many good interview talks and storytelling sessions at his Gardena, California, office and shop. And I hope we have many more yet.

It is further my hope that he would agree that we've become friends. I've written and published books about some of my Hollywood car guy heroes, includ-ing Steve McQueen, Paul Newman, and James Garner. And even though he's a different kind of hero, I promise you that Ed Iskenderian's car guy legend status is no less earned than McQueen's, Garner's, or Newman's.

Ed has enjoyed a long run in the performance industry that grew up because of and around him. His long life and tenure cast a wide net over the speed parts business, stretching from the late 1930s to today. And he knew, was friends with, raced against, or com-peted with the pioneering merchants of speed: Engineering genius and racer Ed Winfield, whom he acknowledges as his primary mentor; Vic Edelbrock (Senior and Junior); Phil Weiand; legendary engine builder Bobby Meeks; and other camshaft innovators and producers, including Chet Herbert, Clay Smith, and Chuck Potvin, plus several members of the Offenhauser family.

Isky is uniquely qualified to recount the history of this movement, the indus-try, and of his company, because *he was there*. When the aftermarket performance industry decided to organize and form a professional trade association in the early 1960s, the membership, composed of his competitors and peers, elected Ed Isken-derian its first president. And he's still an active member.

I've seriously enjoyed putting this book together for you, as I've equally enjoyed getting to know Mr. Isky. I hope you like the result of our BS sessions.

Matt Stone

Chapter 1

IN THE BEGINNING

Two of the Iskenderian brothers, and you'd recognize the mop-headed Ed on the right anywhere. At left is younger brother Luther who is deceased. (Photo Courtesy Ed Iskenderian)

Edward Iskenderian was born July 10, 1921, in Cutler, California, a tiny rural farming town in the Central Valley, near Dinuba and Visalia, in Tulare County. "My father, Dickran, was a blacksmith who emigrated in 1910 from Turkey." He recalls now, "There were too many blacksmiths in California already so that wasn't a good option for him in the New World. My dad somehow had saved up enough money for a down payment on a wine vineyard farm, so at the beginning he was a merchant farmer in America.

"He also worked in a restaurant, helping manage the chickens. They didn't have refrigerator freezers back then, so the restaurant had to maintain a stock of live chickens. When someone ordered a chicken dinner, they'd say, 'Hey Dick [his Americanized name], one chicken!' He'd go back into the cage, catch one and kill it, and then give it to the cook right away, and they'd prepare it while the customers were eating their salad or having drinks.

"My mother, Armine, moved to America in 1919, meeting my father shortly thereafter. Iskenderian is an original Armenian name, stemming from an Eastern European version of Alexander, which read as Iskender, adding the 'ian' to Armenianize the name, thus Iskdenderian. My parents met here in America, through the localized Armenian community, family connections, and so forth [California's central valley had a large Armenian population at the time].

"My family moved to Los Angeles around 1921–1922, not long after my mother immigrated and met and married my dad, and I was born. He'd been in the wine trade near Tulare and suffered near total loss of his crops due to massive winter frost in 1920. So he had to give the farm back to the bank. I was born up there, but we moved to Southern California when I was still a baby. We lived near Pico

Some of the Iskenderian men gather at Abraham Iskenderian's shoe repair shop on Main Street in Visalia, California, circa 1914. Ed's father, Dickran, is seated at left. Dickran's brothers (Ed's uncles) are Abraham (center) and Iskender, also known as Alexander (right). (Photo Courtesy Ed Iskenderian)

and Western in Los Angeles. I have two brothers, Luther, 3 years younger and Ben, 13 years younger.

"There wasn't any demand for blacksmith work in LA at the time, so my dad used what little money he had left to open a shoe repair shop, the same work some of our family members also did in Central California. I remember he used to take me to work with him, and I'd sleep up on a mezzanine above the shop.

"Then we moved to 30th and Main Street, and I went to Jefferson Street School for grammar school. Believe it or not, back in those days we used to have a little shop class in grammar school where we'd begin to learn to work with tools. We got to work with wood, and then later metal. When we were in junior high, we had wood shop, metal shop, and electrical shop, too. And of course in high school there was auto shop. This was great, learning how things worked and working with our hands and with tools. I'm sure this is why I ended up wanting to fix or make things.

From Radios to Cars

"I became very interested in radio and amateur radio. I remember two guys in my homeroom class broadcasting on a 5-meter frequency. They could talk to other amateur radio enthusiasts 10 or even 15 miles away, which I thought was fascinating. So

I went to one of the guy's houses to check out his little homemade radio rig, and he showed me how I could build my own. This was at the dawn of what people later called 'HAM' (or Home Amateur radio operators). These guys didn't have any radio licenses so they made up their own series of call letters and kind of bootlegged their way onto the air. And so did I! This taught me a lot about electricity. I used to repair radios for local people in my neighborhood, for 50 cents or sometimes it was 75 cents if the capacitor was burned out and needed replacing.

"I always enjoyed radios and electrical stuff, but by the time I was a teenager I found cars more interesting. At first, fixing neighbors' radios or bicycles or whatever was how I made money to buy a car and to buy 10-cents-a-gallon gas to drive to the beach with my friends. Remember that at the time (mid-1930s), you used to be able to buy a used Model T for $5 or $10. So once we were old enough to learn how to drive, a lot of us would save up a few dollars from wherever we could earn a buck, and then buy an old Model T.

"These were our first cars, and we learned how to work on them, then we learned, mostly from older guys, how to strip them down and make them go faster. A lot of guys tried to make their cars look like racing cars that we'd see running at board tracks, or pictures in the newspapers of the cars that ran at places like Indianapolis. It turns out that nearly every city and town around Los Angeles had at least a few hot-rodded cars, and some had many.

"Then we heard about a bunch of them running around in the San Fernando Valley, which was up and over the Hollywood Hills and Santa Monica Mountains, an hour or so north of where we all lived. Then some of the guys discovered top-speed racing at the dry lakes, at a place called Muroc (and others), another hour or so north of the Los Angeles basin. Nothing could be more fun back then than having a hopped-up little car like that. They originally called them gow jobs. I don't know why."

Can you imagine *Hot Rod* magazine actually being called *Gow Job* magazine? And of course this nomenclature would have given birth to other titles such as *Popular Gow Jobbing* or everyone would have joined a "gow job club" instead of a hot rod club.

Early Influences

"In our neighborhood there was a guy named Eugene and another nick-named Baldy. They were older and more advanced in building cars. Our local Los Angeles–based hot rod club was called the Bungholers. You may wonder about the name. Well, even when we weren't out racing or working on someone's car, we'd get together and hang out at the electrical shop that belonged to one of the member's family, and his father used to come out and see us all hanging around talking about girls and cars, and he'd say, 'All you guys just sit around like a bunch of ass-holes!' Well, we thought the principle was kinda funny but didn't think it would be a good idea to have jackets or club plaques made up in the name of the 'A***olers car club' so we adopted 'Bungholers.'"

I asked Isky if he ever felt any preju-dice from the hot rod racing and car club gang about his being Armenian. He said, "No, there were a few other Armenian guys around, as well as Japanese and Mexi-can, and nobody seemed to care. Most of my friends were Jewish guys. Although I remember one time we were swimming in the reservoir at the Sunset Fields golf course in Culver City. This was the reser-voir water they irrigated the lawns with, but the security guy chewed us out a little saying he didn't want any Armenians swimming or peeing in their drinking water, and of course the funny part was that it wasn't their drinking water, it was only for irrigation."

Although it's interesting that later on, there were a couple of pretty success-ful racers of Armenian descent, one of them named John Mazmanian, another East Coaster named Seto Postoian, and of course, Mike "Blackie" Gejeian, a noted racer, hot rodder, and car builder also from Central California.

John Athan(asopolis)

"In grammar school, I met a kid named Jimmy Pierson. He was a good guy and we became friends. We used to go home from school about the same way, and he lived with a guy named John Athan, who was a year older than I was. Or I should more accurately say that John Athan lived with him. Some of the immi-grant names were cumbersome for Amer-icans to pronounce, so often, they'd be shortened, either officially or just unof-ficially so they were easier to remember or pronounce. John's family came from Greece, so his father shortened their name from Athanasopolis to just Athan. Our name was never officially shortened from Iskenderian, but from early on I was nick-named Isky.

"Jimmy's mother and John's mother worked together in a restaurant, but for some reason, John's mother made a lot less money and couldn't afford to raise and take care of John, so he lived with the Pearsons and Mrs. Athan paid them a little money to help with their expenses.

"As we got older, John had Model Ts and he knew more about them than

A young John Athan with his Model T–bodied, Essex-framed, hopped-up 4-cylinder hot rod, circa 1936. Note the long, open, mufflerless exhaust system that Isky recalls "made a beautiful sound." This is the car he'd soon sell to Ed without the Ford bodywork, because Ed felt he could find another body for $3 less. And he did! (Photo Courtesy Ed Iskenderian)

Friends then and friends now. John Athan is the tall, lanky kid on the left, Isky is the man at right, with an unidentified friend in the middle. Upon John's discharge from the Navy in 1946, the three met up in Detroit to check out the car scene then head to Indianapolis Motor Speedway for the first post–World War II running of the Indy 500. (Photo Courtesy Ed Iskenderian)

the rest of us did; how to hop them up and make them faster. So we talked and learned about Rajo and Fronty (Frontenac) racing cylinder heads, hotter camshafts, and other performance tricks and equipment. We both happened to have the same Phillips bicycles. John was more advanced in terms of machines and doing machine

work than the rest of us. But as we got further into cars and wanted to do more to them, John taught a lot of us how, and sometimes we could even do the work at school in the machine shop or auto shop.

"For some reason, our young community of hot rodders was very unselfish with their experience and knowledge about cars. I don't know if they just liked to feel like they were more adult by helping out the younger guys, or if they really wanted to keep us from making some of the mistakes they made. Keep in mind that getting a job in a machine shop was tough during the Depression, but once World War II started, there was demand for good fabricators, machinists, and tool and die makers. You could get a job doing machine work earning 50 cents an hour back then. By then, I was 18 or 19, and worked in a machine shop, and really began to learn about how to work on things. John was not only a very good machinist, but a gifted draftsman."

Suffice it to say that Athan and young Ed Iskenderian became fast (and ultimately lifelong) friends. They messed around with cars together, raced together, and traveled together. Just prior to World War II, Ed bought John's Model T–based hot rod when John became tired of the unreliable nature of its hopped-up, highly tuned Model T engine. Ed had his own plans for the little black roadster, as you'll see in the

John Athan's second Ford hot rod, after the early Model T car he sold to Isky. This may have very well been the first "AV-8" rod built; it is the mating of a Model A body mounted atop a '32 Ford chassis, retaining the flathead Ford V-8 and a '32 Ford grille shell and radiator. If so, it's a timeless style that's been copied countless times, and still looks just right. Athan, being an accomplished artist and draftsman, had a good eye for design and nailed the stance, proportions, colors, and look of this car.

The detailing is also superb, with the red-painted wire wheels, and shiny running hubcaps and trim rings. Note the beautiful, seamless, flowing one-piece windshield frame; it's positively elegant. Apparently the look also appealed to the movie studio that produced Elvis Presley's 1957 film Loving You. A brooding Presley drove the car with aplomb, and it sounded great.

The car is seen here on display at the Smithsonian Institution's American History Museum. It is mostly original, having been restored by Athan some decades ago. (Photo Courtesy Bob Collum)

Athan's flathead V-8 is a textbook example of the flathead art of the 1950s, although it runs factory Ford cast-iron heads instead of the more common aftermarket aluminum pieces. The dual-carb manifold is an Edelbrock slingshot; also note the highly stylized machined intake stakes. The car's detailing is superb, as evidenced by the chromed tube exhaust headers and chromed water tubes. Along the way, the generator has been updated to a later production piece. This look has inspired countless hundreds of hot rod roadster builds and still looks just right today. (Photo Courtesy Bob Collum)

next chapter. Ed ultimately launched his performance camshaft business from the back room of John's machine shop, and as of this writing, the pair have known each other for 87 years. It was in the back room of Athan's original tool and die shop where Iskenderian opened his high-performance camshaft company, with one employee and one grinding machine.

Not long after selling his Model T–based hot rod to Isky, Athan built another rod, this time with a Model A body set atop '32 Ford frame rails, running its flat-head Ford V-8.

This seminal black-and-red roadster is considered by many to be the first ever constructed, or among the first, hot rod nicknamed an "AV-8," meaning of course a Model A body with a '32 Ford V-8 chassis and powertrain. It is the very definition of a traditional American Ford-based hot rod, the look, stance, and performance so right that the car appeared in many movies. Among its most famous appearances was in the 1957 Elvis Presley film, *Loving You.* The car is as big a star as The King himself, featured prominently with Elvis driving it in several scenes, its throaty V-8 rumble heard clearly in the soundtrack.

As of this writing, Athan still owns the car. The curators of the Smithsonian Institution's American History Museum felt that it was such a definitive example of the hot rod genre that it lived for more than a decade on display at the Museum, along-side a vintage Harley-Davidson motorcycle and a Greyhound Scenicruiser bus as examples of uniquely American forms of transportation.

Athan recalls that he "wanted to live the hot rod lifestyle, and that he did." He did so by living in Southern California, building and racing his own cars. Isky recalls that hundreds of [mostly female] fans had written fan letters to Elvis Presley in care of the studio during the filming of *Loving You*, and that dozens of the letters were still in the car when filming wrapped and the car was returned to Athan. The sad news is that Athan didn't see any interest or value in Elvis's discarded fan mail, so he just threw it all away.

As of this writing, Isky and Athan still have lunch together every Wednesday at their favorite burger joint in South Los Angeles.

Ed Winfield

"As we got deeper and deeper into cars, we met and learned about Ed Winfield, born in 1900, who was a racing driver. He was known as a real wizard when it came to hopping up cars and motorcycles," Isky recalls. "He knew how to make hot cam-shafts and even built his own carburetors too. I bought my first cam from Winfield. One of the most amazing stories I recall

A smiling young Ed Winfield aboard his stripped-down Model T Raceabout. Given the amount of dirt and the smile on his face, he must have done very well in his race. Note the well-dressed crowd around his car; when was the last time you wore a suit and a bowtie to a dirt track motor race? (Photo Courtesy Ed Iskenderian)

about Winfield, who lived up in the La Cañada and Flintridge area, just over the hills north of downtown Los Angeles, was that one time he was riding his bicycle out in the countryside near his home when a man rode up in a horse and buggy and stopped to talk to another man who was there, telling him that he just heard the news that San Francisco was on fire."

This, of course, was in 1906, at the beginning of the great San Francisco earthquake and fire. "Winfield was about six years old at the time, very smart, and by the age of four or five had fully taught himself how to read and write. Naturally, this was major news at the time that a whole city could be burning. We'd never heard of such a thing.

Ed Winfield, a tall, slender gent, is seen here working in his Flintridge area shop, where he not only ground camshafts but also modified heads, built entire engines, and produced carburetors. Isky, over time, produced engine accessories and systems ancillary to camshafts as well as valvetrain hardware (including supercharger drives, timing chains and gears, and more). (Photo Courtesy Ed Iskenderian)

A young, goggled Ed Winfield in his Model T racer. Note the single seat and small round fuel tank mounted just aft of the driver. Although we don't know with absolute certainty, it's likely that this photo was snapped in the mid-1920s at Gilmore Stadium in Los Angeles, a place where Winfield raced often and well. The two long exhaust pipes indicate the T was assuredly powered by one of his highly modified 4-cylinders with two "two-into-one" exhaust manifolds. Winfield's attire was common for the day, long before Nomex fire suits fully emblazoned with sew-on sponsor patches. The car wears no sponsor stickers either, and the race numbers were painted onto the radiator grille visible only from the front. The proper young gent racer wore only a tie and vest. (Photo Courtesy Ed Iskenderian)

"Winfield always wanted to learn about cars and anything mechanical, so also at about that time when he was just five or six years old, he used to write a penny postcard to the car manufacturers asking them for information about their new models (remembering that this was just at the dawn of the automotive age), and the car companies used to send him brochures and flyers about their new cars and their engineering advancements. Winfield was always ahead of his time."

By 1912, he had his first motorcycle, and of course, immediately went to work figuring out how to make it go faster. He went on to become a self-taught engineer and racing driver and lived most of his life custom-building camshafts and carburetors out of a small garage-size shop for a variety of racing teams. The shop had no signage or any other hints of the work that went on within.

He was also a highly successful Model T racer, competing at most Southern California venues, sometimes against big name pros. He was well known around local racing circles and was often covered in the newspapers. Winfield won his share with clever home-built cars and was famously innovative when it came to working over camshafts, heads, and carburetors. During his life, he worked for racing great, car designer and builder Harry Miller and consulted with several Detroit automakers on their high-performance engine developments.

Ed Iskenderian acknowledges Ed Winfield as one of his inspirations for getting into the high-performance equipment business, as his primary mentor, and a friend until the latter's passing in 1980. Iskenderian still owns Winfield's original cam-grinding machine.

"We never knew what a cam-grinding machine looked like. Winfield built his own out of a cylindrical grinding machine, and he showed it to my friends and me. Later on when I decided to try my hand at developing and machining performance camshafts, he showed me how to convert a cylindrical grinder into a cam grinder. He was very unselfish with his time and knowledge, probably because he knew that a young guy like me that knew next to nothing was never going to be any kind of competitor to him. I don't know that he ever made much money in his life. A couple of times he hired others to mass produce some of his components, but not much ever came of that. But the underground racing network knew his reputation far and wide."

Isky recalls that after he'd already set up his own camshaft grinding shop, he felt a little guilty that he might be horning in on Winfield's turf a little bit. But he tempered that concern with the knowledge that several other guys had recently entered the performance cam business, and they all had plenty of work. Moreover, because "none of us were as smart at this as Winfield was, we couldn't possibly damage his business." He adds that Ed

Young Airman Ed Iskenderian never achieved his dream of being an Army Air Corps pilot, which certainly kept him out of harm's way during World War II. Ed attributed his survival of the war to "the Man Upstairs having a higher calling for him, or perhaps someday God decided He might need a cam for a flathead." (Photo Courtesy Ed Iskenderian)

What Is a Camshaft Anyway?

Any racer or engine builder will likely agree that the camshaft (or in some cases, multiple camshafts) is/are the heartbeat of the engine. Webster's defines a camshaft as a noun: *a shaft that has cams attached to it, forming part of a mechanical device.* The camshaft is a shaft made up of a variety of concentric "lobes"; the shaft is connected via chains, gears, or belts to the engine's crankshaft and ignition systems, all of which make up some of an engine's reciprocating componentry. The camshaft's primary responsibility is to open and close the engine's intake and exhaust valves in a specific order to draw atomized fuel and air into the engine's combustion chambers, and then allow for its escape in a proper sequence.

All street performance engines are four-stroke engines, for the most part, meaning that four distinct events (or "strokes") must occur within a cylinder for the engine to make power. The first stroke is the intake stroke, where the piston is moving down in the cylinder and is drawing an air/fuel mixture into that cylinder. It is able to do that because the intake valve is open, as dictated by that cylinder's intake lobe on the camshaft.

After that, the assembly rotates further, reversing piston direction and moving it back up in the cylinder, compressing the air/fuel mixture that was recently drawn in. The mixture is compressing because the camshaft has dictated that both valves are closed during this sequence. When the mixture is fully compressed, spark from the ignition system ignite this volatile compressed air/fuel mixture to force the piston down in the cylinder bore with great force, which is the third sequence in this four-stroke cycle. The valves remain closed for this sequence as well.

In the fourth and final stroke, through inertia and momentum from the power stroke, the piston once again rises in the cylinder bore. The difference this time is that the camshaft has opened the exhaust valve, which allows the escape of all the spent gases left over from the power stroke. In polite terms, the four-stroke cycle is referred to as 1 = Intake, 2 = Compression, 3 = Power, 4 = Exhaust. Hot rodders often refer to it more crudely as suck, squeeze, bang, blow. Crude yes, but easy to remember.

You might think of the camshaft as the precision choreographer of all the critical timing between air, fuel, compression, combustion, and exhaust. The camshaft is often referred to as "the heart of the engine," as its design is the most influential component of engine behavior.

The size and shape of those lobes, which control the opening and closing of the engine's intake and exhaust valves, can be varied greatly to impact the power output, performance, smoothness, emissions, and fuel economy of an engine. After the young hot rodders figured out that developing camshaft lobe profiles that modulated the actions of the valves in differing ways actually had a huge impact on engine performance, the notion of performance cam grinding was born.

Without getting overly technical, changes in camshaft lobe profiles, often in conjunction with raising the cylinders' compression ratio, and revising carburetion or fuel and air intake, could often enhance the engine's "volumetric efficiency" to create more power. Mechanical brainiacs Clay Smith and Ed Winfield realized this early on, which is how they began developing "racing cams" to sell to the dry lakes crowd that was in search of power and speed. Iskenderian and a host of others soon followed them into this burgeoning business. It was based on more and more research, new ideas, trial and error, having little fear of being wrong, and not worrying about blowing up an engine now and again.

About the meaning of all this, Ed is quoted in the March 2014 issue of *Hot Rod DELUXE*, "There's a lot of expensive stuff on the market, and I wonder if a guy starting out gets confused and spends money on the wrong stuff. The first thing we learned from Winfield was volumetric efficiency. We didn't know what that was at the time, but learned that if you could fill the cylinder [with atomized fuel and air] 100 percent, that's 100 percent efficiency. So I'm thinking the average guy might spend a lot of money on stuff he doesn't need and should be advised some of the stuff he could do with his stock engine, like a cam and carburetion alone."

It's the concentric lobes on a camshaft that help orchestrate the mathematically intricate relationship between the intake, compression, ignition, and exhaust phases of four-cycle construction, and keep the crankshaft, pistons, valves, and ignition systems all speaking to each other in time. (Photo Courtesy Mel Stone)

Winfield told him, "If you had told me that you really wanted to get into this as a business and not just as a hobby, I would have helped you out a lot more." Isky says Ed was "one of the smartest people I ever met, the old master of camshaft science, and I wouldn't have made it into the business without knowing him and without his help."

Ed continued to build and develop his metalworking and machining skills throughout high school and post-graduation, and made money doing a variety of small machine work jobs. But like many young Americans at the dawn of World War II, he sensed a higher calling and wanted to defend his country and learn more about mechanical things. So he enlisted in the Army Air Corps, which of course became the Air Force some years later.

Young Iskenderian's experience in the corps was mixed. He wanted to be a pilot in the worst way, but had to acknowledge that he became airsick easily, and made more than a few of his flight instructors nervous. It was clear that his career as a

fighter pilot wasn't to be, even though with practice he ultimately got past those two situations.

At about this same time, the Allied Forces were winning the war and demand for newly trained combat pilots reduced substantially. He was then transferred to the Air Transport Command, finishing out the war working cargo and transport duty in the Pacific Islands. He wasn't piloting the plane, but at least he was flying, and that counted for something. Plus he learned a lot about how aircraft were engineered and built.

After a while, his main job was as somewhat of a "steward" to any military personnel who were catching a ride to and from various deployments. He took this assignment sort of hard, considering himself a "washout" from the Air Corps. After his discharge near the end of World War II, Iskenderian came home to Los Angeles to finish up the hot rod he'd bought from friend John Athan in the mid-1930s. He also had to get to work on a career, and ultimately a family and a business of his own.

Vic Edelbrock Sr. at the wheel of his own fast, record-setting 1932 Ford roadster ready to run on the California dry lake beds. Vic's car is well prepared and stripped of all non-essentials, including the convertible top, fenders, running boards, bumpers, and lighting. Anything that added weight or could slow the airflow over the car likely spent the weekend sitting on the lakebed floor. Edelbrock's car is typical of many cars that ran at the dry lakes, although likely better prepared and always immaculate. (Photo Courtesy Edelbrock LLC)

The Hot Rod Scene

California's hot rod scene was in full swing by the time Isky mustered out of the Army; tens of thousands of young vets returned from the service with the desire of making cars go fast, and many of them had some money in their pockets with which to pursue the car scene and speed. Hot rodding was born in California, particularly in Southern California, although seedlings of speed were popping up in the Midwest and on the East Coast as well. The science of going faster, be it over a measured distance, such as a mile or a quarter of a mile, or for top speed, was in its infancy. Very few "aftermarket" parts were available for most cars, even though this business had begun to develop in the 1930s. The bits that were available were high-priced racing parts engineered primarily to fit Ford Model T and Model A 4-cylinder engines.

A typical Edelbrock-modified flathead Ford V-8 with Edelbrock high-compression heads, tubular headers, and dual Stromberg carbs atop an Edelbrock dual-carb intake manifold. Immaculate in every way. (Photo Courtesy Edelbrock LLC)

By the mid-1930s, Ford had launched its affordable, flexible "flathead V-8" engine, and Chevrolet and others had big inline 6s that out-powered the old, low-tech Ford 4s. Most of the secrets of going faster came by trial and error, with more than a few blown-up engines along the way. In the early days, most improvements in speed or acceleration performance came from "stripping the car down" by removing items unnecessary for making speed. Reducing weight had an effect similar to making more power, and taking off heavy parts, such as fenders, rear seats, headlights, and windshields, was free; exotic "speed parts" cost a lot of money. This scene, and from experience in the military, is where the young hot rodders learned the baseline notions of "streamlining" and the effect that wind resistance and aerodynamic drag had on a car as it sped across the lakebed in search of a higher top speed.

It is often said that the notion of car racing dates back to the building of the second automobile, the theory being that the instant any two cars met on the road or at an intersection, the natural inclination of the two cars' drivers was to "run 'em" to see whose car was faster. The *Chicago-Times Herald* Race of 1895 is widely acknowledged as the first organized motorsports event in America.

The seminal Indianapolis 500 dates back to 1911. Drag racing wasn't formally organized until the birth of the NHRA in 1951, but, of course, street racing had become popular and somewhat notorious by the 1930s. Yet top speed meets, run on several deserted dry lakebeds north and east of Los Angeles, had also sprung up, and these "timing run meets" were held several times a year, sanctioned, or at least put together, by a network of Los Angeles and San Fernando Valley–based hot rod clubs.

The Dry Lakes

The Muroc Racing Association (MRA) held its first meet on the Muroc dry lakebed in May 1932. Why a dry lakebed such as Muroc? The reasons are straightforward; the dry lakebed surface was relatively smooth and depending on the weather, packed pretty hard. And these great lakebeds ran for miles, allowing most cars time and distance to run up to full speed,

plus a "cool down" mile at the end of the run to slow down.

And of course, there were no speed limits on this largely unregulated, unpatrolled, massively large bit of desert. It was important that there were no pedestrians, buildings, schools, or rows of trees or homes to hit; nor police enforcement and interference. It was wide-open desert, so these spots were considered safer than attempting to run any sort of top-speed competition on public roads. Safer than running more than 100 mph on a public road? Yes, but ultimately safe? Maybe not so much.

Author Robert Genat notes in his fine book, *The Birth of Hot Rodding: The Story of the Dry Lakes Era*, that "Early MRA meets were loosely organized with as many as five cars running across the lakebed at one time. Only the driver of the front-running car had a clear view ahead. Those trailing behind were lost in the billowing clouds of dust that the leaders created."

Other organizations formed to hold similar top-speed meets, such as the Southern California Timing Association (SCTA) and the Western Timing Association (WTA), to run at El Mirage, Rosamond, and a few other desert locales. Today, most of

The Muroc train station depot, as illustrated on this book by William Carroll, was about the only thing that marked the location. Note the timetable on the wall, which gives estimated arrival and departure times for both eastbound and westbound trains. Muroc was one of several dry lakebeds that the racers used to run for top speed, and it was the favorite of many. The racing, like this building, are long gone; the property belongs to the U.S. government and has long been annexed into what is now Edwards Air Force Base near Rosamond, California.

Two "gow jobs" stripped of non-essentials are ready to make their runs for Velocity Maximum, or top speed. (Photo Courtesy Ed Iskenderian)

The action was a little wild and woolly at times as cars took off across the lakebed either warming up or just screwing around. Here's one going not quite straight, practicing a little of what we now call drifting in the soft sand of the lakebed. (Photo Courtesy Ed Iskenderian)

these have been annexed by the military under the auspices of what is now Edwards Air Force Base, near Rosamond, California.

"Those early days at the dry lakes were pretty wild and woolly," notes veteran racer, automotive journalist, and book author Tom Madigan. "A lot of times, guys were just so anxious to run or wanted to shake down and test their car that they'd just pull out on the course and go for it, sometimes running head to head with other guys, tearing around in all directions."

Of course there were accidents and casualties, but the sport progressed as the timing associations developed course controls and codes of conduct for these events, often insisting that drivers, car owners,

and any other attendees sign documents containing these rules of behavior before they were allowed to run. The conditions weren't very hospitable either; there were no hotels about, so camping or simply sleeping in your car or on the ground was the norm. There was invariably a hastily constructed timing and scoring tower, and several of the clubs developed equipment to accurately measure a car's top speed over a given distance. Remember, unlike drag racing, this was only about top speed at the time; 0–60 mph or quarter-mile acceleration times were not yet the common matrices of competition.

This racing grew in popularity throughout the 1930s, and of course came to an

In the early days, any guy and his car were pretty much defined by the club they hung with. These cast "club plates" told everyone your colors. Today, original examples of these cast aluminum plates are highly prized and can be quite costly for those who want to run them on vintage rods.

abrupt end at the dawn of World War II because most of the young male competitors went into the service. However, it all came back with a vengeance in 1946, with so many young men returning from military service with a heightened appreciation for cars and how to make them go faster. Many had learned machining and mechanical skills in the service, and they all had a little "mustering out" pay in their pockets to spend on building hotter, faster cars.

Young Ed Iskenderian, John Athan, and their pals were all part of this scene, before and after The Big War. Isky has fond memories of those times. Their Bungholers club was too small to host and stage timed events at Muroc, but they certainly participated.

What club you belonged to was very much a matter of prestige and a badge of honor. Los Angeles' Road Runners was one of the most prestigious of the hot rod clubs at the time and there were dozens of others (with charming automotively related

names such as the Strokers, the Smokers, and the Trompers); if you belonged to one, you likely ran a license plate–sized cast aluminum "club plate" somewhere on your car, and probably also had a club "letterman's" jacket to advertise your club patronage.

Isky recalls that "we tried to leave Los Angeles for the lakes on a Friday afternoon, so we could get up there, stake out a good camping spot, and get working on our cars. Or sometimes we'd drive up on Saturday in advance of the timed runs taking place on Sunday. It was a lot of fun, but very dusty of course, and it sure got cold out there on the desert floor at night. Some guys set up tents, but most of us just slept on the ground, or if you were a smaller guy like me, you could sleep in your car.

"We also used to bring our own food and water, because once you were out there, there was no place to get it. No Starbucks on the corner, or McDonald's drive-thru. Although a couple of

"Line 'em up!" This group of stripped-down gow jobs is ready to assault the lakebed. Car nos. 9 and 111 are '32 Ford roadsters, while car no. 4, the third in line, is a Model A. The fabulous Deuce is as handsome a hot rod as ever created, but if it has a downside, it's that it is a rather tall visage and has a fair amount of aerodynamic drag. Even so, resourceful rodders and racers improved the '32's aero prospects with careful ride height adjustments, the removal of non-essentials, and careful blocking of the front radiator grille opening. (Photo Courtesy Pat Ganahl)

enterprising folks sold coffee and donuts or sandwiches out of a car or truck."

There were no highly developed pit areas either; you'd just gather with your

You can just about hear this conversation through the span of time. "Hmm. Wonder what happened? Hey, is that piston rod supposed to be hanging out of the side of this engine block?" Or, "Wonder if we crank up the timing a little more and take the cooling fan off the engine, if it'll go any faster?" Guys in white T-shirts learning their way around the game of speed. (Photo Courtesy Ed Iskenderian)

friends, stake out a spot, and get to work on your car. Isky recalls this being "mostly a man's sport," although some of the guys brought wives and girlfriends along. Most of the drivers were men too, although there were a few women, most notably Veda Orr, wife of speed shop owner Karl Orr, who had her own race car, drove well, and set many records.

If there's any visual of this scene, it's a small group of guys wearing Levis and white T-shirts gathered around the engine compartment of a Model T, trying to get it ready to run, make it go faster, or (all too often) figure out why it blew up.

The whole scene was still in its infancy and so much of what made a car run faster, slower, or not at all was trial and error. There were very few "speed parts" that you could get or afford. No highly developed automotive performance aftermarket existed as it does today, although sometimes, expensive, pedigreed pure racing cars showed up to have their shot at the lakebed.

Many of the cars were very casually built, with little attention paid to their "show quality" shine or chrome levels. This husky-looking Model T–bucket body wears a "raceabout-style" racing fuel tank, a grille shell of unknown manufacture, and a beefy-looking flathead with an early Edelbrock "slingshot" manifold and a pair of Stromberg carbs. The driver already looks a little sunburned and tired, as if he's already made a few long hot runs on the lakebed. (Photo Courtesy Pat Ganahl)

This big Deuce stands tall and proud, its driver happy and ready to run, or perhaps satisfied with the run he just completed. He must be running an Isky cam, as the photo is autographed "Regards to Ed, & Thanks from Mac." This great shot is dated June 25, 1933, at Muroc. (Photo Courtesy Ed Iskenderian)

It was at the dry lakes, and certainly in other organized forms of racing, such as stadium and board track racing, that the first kernels of the aftermarket performance industry were born, because so many of them (the original "merchants of speed") were out there at the dry lakes, with cars, ingenuity, and ideas: Vic Edelbrock Sr., Stu Hillborn, engine builder Bobby Meeks, Fred Carillo, Mickey Thompson, Alex Xydias, Veda and Karl Orr, Ak Miller, Wally Parks, Otto Crocker, Phil Weiand, Clay Smith, and countless others

who played pivotal roles in the birth of the aftermarket performance industry.

Ed also recalls the occasional appearance by young, wealthy Los Angeles playboy Tommy Lee, whose father Don Lee was a luxury car dealer in Los Angeles. Ed remembers when Lee the younger showed up at the lakes with a Bugatti, "which was about the most exotic street car I'd ever seen," Isky now recalls. "Somehow, one time, he lost control of the car (I think a wheel broke) and I remember that expensive Bugatti sitting there in the dirt, all smashed up, but fortunately Tommy wasn't hurt. And seeing all those beautiful machined aluminum wheels all busted up too."

Some slightly strange scanning and printing have distorted the proportions of this pit area shot; not everybody was this unnaturally long and tall at the time, but it gives you an idea of the crowds that gathered for a "timing event" weekend, as well as the looks and diversity of cars that showed up to run. Isky isn't 100 percent sure of the location but believes it was at Muroc. (Photo Courtesy Ed Iskenderian)

Chapter 2

THE ISKY ROADSTER

A dashing, young Ed Iskenderian with his freshly finished T/V-8 roadster on the streets of Los Angeles, likely just after completing his service in the U.S. Army Air Corps. The car, and the guy, have great a stance, cutting classic profiles. Note the DIVCO Helms bakery delivery truck at left, a common site in Southern California at the time. Helms was based in Culver City, home to several of Iskenderian's shops in the early days, when bakeries delivered bread and milk to your doorstep. (Photo Courtesy Ed Iskenderian)

What would a hot rodder be without a great hot rod? Ed Iskenderian's now famous Model T/V-8 wasn't his first car, but it came pretty early in his automotive game.

Isky was born in 1921, so by the time he was of driving age in the mid-1930s, the Ford Model T had come and gone from production, as had the Model A. The 1932 and later flathead V-8–powered Fords were the performance leaders on the affordable new-car scene, with the older, slower, less advanced 4-cylinder Model Ts and As being somewhat less desirable. They were both cheap and plentiful as used cars and also still popular as hot rods and racing cars.

"It used to be," recalls Isky, "that you could walk into any large parking lot and find a used Model T for sale for $5 or maybe $10 for a good one. We were kids in the early post-Depression era and didn't have much money, so that's what we all bought for our first cars, and then of course tried to figure out how to make them go faster without spending money we didn't have."

Teenaged Ed made a few dollars here and there repairing AM radios belonging to neighbors and friends. It was mostly replacing tubes and repairing broken electrical wires or connections. In addition, he had the occasional odd job as a machinist apprentice.

Here are two very different iterations of the Athan-Iskenderian roadster; the top photo of a teenage John Athan with the car still configured with a Rajo-headed 4-banger, its original champ car–style exhaust, and first Ford Model T "turtle deck" bodywork. The bottom shot shows the same car with Isky aboard, the 4-banger now replaced with a stock 1936 Ford flathead V-8 and junkyard fresh, although it has virtually identical bodywork. Note that the engine runs stock heads and a single carburetor; the wheels are still black. (Photos Courtesy Ed Iskenderian)

A Frankenstein of Sorts

Ed did not initially build from scratch the car that we now call the Isky Roadster. Ed's childhood (and now lifelong) friend, John Athan owned it before Ed. Even then Athan wasn't the original owner; that was another acquaintance of theirs named Buzz Johnson. And even though it's often referred to as a "Model T" with the exception of its Ford "turtle deck" bodywork, there isn't a huge amount of Model T left in it.

Isky recalls that "it's built on late 1920s Essex frame rails; nice because these rails are very flat and smooth on top without a lot of curves in the chassis, which allows you to mount nearly any kind of body, suspension, and powertrain onto them relatively easily without a lot of metal work to make stuff fit. The steering was off an air-cooled Franklin, as was the original front axle, although with no front brakes. The body was from a mid-1920s Model T, with a Ford Model B 4-cylinder engine running a Rajo head. It had a big, long header and exhaust pipe on it that ran high along

Recall that Isky's roadster was built on Essex frame rails. Never heard of an Essex? Here's one in a vintage photo taken on the streets of downtown Los Angeles in the late 1920s. Essex automobiles were produced by the Essex Motor Company between 1918 and 1922 and then by Hudson Motor Company of Detroit, Michigan, between 1922 and 1933. The man leaning on the doorframe is unidentified, but the dapper gent in the rumble seat is the author's maternal grandfather, Harry Platt, who never drove but loved automobiles nonetheless.

the driver's side of the body (not so very different than that on an Indy racing roadster of the period, which may have inspired it), and it made a beautiful sound."

Ed also recalls that Athan ran the car with a borrowed high-performance magneto ignition that belonged to another friend, and that every time John wanted to race the car, he had to borrow this magneto, run the car, and then return it. One can only wonder what he did when the magneto system wasn't available; just push the car down the street or run a stock lower-voltage system?

Additional hardware included a Ruxtell 2-speed rear end and Western Auto Center (a then-popular chain of auto parts and service stores that competed with Pep Boys) Air Cooled tires. They weren't really air cooled, in the sense of an aircraft or Volkswagen engine. But they did have deep ridges molded into the sidewall at the outer edges of the treads sort of resembling cooling fins, so it made for a catchy brand name.

"I think John bought this car from Buzz for something like $25 and made a

Although Isky built his car primarily for speed, it boasts a classy cabin. The instrument panel is classic Auburn (as are the gauges), still so sought after by hot rod builders. The An innovative triangle-shaped mount that also houses the tach supports the "banjo" steering wheel's column. The shifter stirs a '32 Ford 3-speed manual transmission, and the cabin was stitched in firm, deeply grained oxblood-colored leather, which has faded to a warm brown after nearly 70 years.

few changes along the way. He decided he wanted front brakes, so he bought a '32 Ford front axle with suspension and brakes." He grafted it onto the roadster in the name of (he hoped) safer braking when going fast.

Isky Gets Started

"One day, John took off with the car running on all four cylinders and came back with a dead engine. He'd either thrown a piston rod or broke the crankshaft, and kinda became disgusted with the car, so he sold it off in a couple of major pieces. He sold what was left of the engine to one guy, and I bought the rest of the car but not the body. John sold me the frame, wheels, and running gear for $25, but he wanted an extra $10 for the Model T body, which I thought was too much. So I found another body in a boneyard for $7, which saved me $3. This was fine because I had no interest in the previous engine, since my plan was to upgrade the car to a Ford flathead V-8."

This transaction took place in 1938, and Isky also recalls that a used late-1936 Ford flathead V-8 cost about $65 in a wrecking yard at the time. He doesn't even recall how he raised that much money back then. With no modifications, the small, lightweight roadster ran at least 90-mph top speed with no problem. "It may have been a stock flathead, but to me, a kid who

You could call this a CLMSL, for Center Low-Mounted Stop Light. This was typical of many cars of the 1920s; there were no flashing turn signals, and rear running and brake lighting consisted of a single fixture.

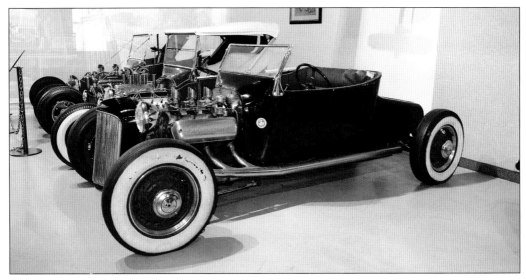

The Isky Roadster takes pride of place among many other hot rodding and drag racing greats at the NHRA Wally Parks Museum in Pomona, California. The tires are at least 60 years old, and the oil in the engine may be the same.

grew up with flathead Model T 4-cylinder engines, it looked like a racing engine!"

He also found the Model T "turtle deck" body he was looking for and put the car together with a stock 1936 Ford flathead V-8. "Back then, the late 1936 flathead was the engine to have. It used the best materials, had the highest horsepower rating, and was the easiest to modify and make faster." So that was the first V-8 that Isky found and installed in the car. He started out running it with a single carbu-

retor, then dual Strombergs, then ultimately a set of semi-exotic Maxi heads; he experimented with a wide variety of intake and carb solutions.

More modifications included a beautiful machine-turned metal dashboard out of an Auburn, then and still a popular hot rod instrument panel because it is not only racy- and sporty-looking, but offers very complete instrumentation with plenty of

It would take sharp and knowledgeable eyes to recognize this unusual grille as two top halves of a Pontiac grille that have been welded together. The tall, angled headlight stanchions are hand fabricated and angled such to give the car a charming, slightly googly-eyed face.

The Isky Roadster hasn't been street licensed for decades, and its six-decade-old black lacquer paint is checked and cracked, yet still has a certain shiny/dull warm glow about it. The turtle deck body is terminally cute, with no trunk or rumble seat. A hand-fabbed exhaust system was among the car's final finishing touches when construction was complete.

The roadster "rode pretty well on smooth Los Angeles roads at the time, but bucked like a bronco on Mexico's rutted pavement or dirt roads," prompting Isky to seek out dampening, something that previous owner Athan never installed on the car. These are period Houdaille lever action shocks, which Isky had reconfigured to a "50/50 action," meaning equal levels of compression and rebound.

gauge pods. It didn't, however, contain a spot for a tachometer, so a special binnacle was built to house the tach, and the same piece also serves as the steering column mounting bracket.

This car proved to be the template for a Model T Ford pre– and immediate post–World War II hot rod. Ed had plans to modify the car further in the name of more speed but was at first content to run the car with the pretty much stock V-8. He took it on an epic road trip to Mexico with a group of friends in 1940.

Among the more memorable aspects of this adventure were the country's horrible road conditions, and the Model T's pounding ride, because it had no shock absorbers. It was so bad, Ed was afraid that the suspension or frame would crack. After a while, he parked the roadster at someone's house in Mexico and rode along in another more conventional car, vowing to source and engineer some dampening upon his return to Los Angeles. When he was home, he hit the junkyards in search of something that would quell the T's rib-shaking body motions.

Ed was pleased to find a set of Houdaille (pronounced "Oooh-die") hydraulic lever action shocks from "some expensive car or other, because they were preferred by many premium luxury and sports car makers" of the time. He found a guy who rebuilt shock absorbers and had the Houdailles freshened and recalibrated for a "50/50" action, meaning equal dampening on the compression and release stroke. They did the trick, substantially improving the car's ride and handling.

Dry Lakes Testing and Tuning

Ed also recalls one slightly harrowing ride he took early on with the car. He and Athan took it to the Muroc dry lakes to test out the new engine and some modifications. When previously installing the '32 Ford axle and brakes, Athan elected to modify the axle and frame to accept a set of semi-elliptical springs, instead of the '32 Ford's stock transverse leaf setup. John fabricated a set of pad-like mounting brackets to adapt these springs to his frame and axle. However, they were brazed onto the front of the car using a relatively soft brass brazing material, instead of more robust fusing steel-to-steel welding.

Prior to their trip to the dry lakes, Isky noticed that some of the brazing had begun to crack but "hadn't spread too far." But during a test run on a service road running parallel to the Muroc dry lake speed course, the front axle broke off. Isky was driving the car, wearing a borrowed helmet. He remembers that this was a likely military surplus open face canvas or leather helmet; there was no thought of seat belts, roll bars, or any sort of fire suit or other safety gear.

Luckily, Isky was able to keep the car under control with minimal damage and neither of the hapless young occupants was hurt. It could have been Isky's last ride, the notion of which Isky chuffs by saying, "Perhaps the Man Upstairs might have thought He'd need a camshaft someday, so I was spared."

"Every time we went out and drove the car or ran it for top speed, we learned

This unique radiator mascot and grille shell badge identify this as the one and only Isky Roadster. Note the handsome machine-turned and polished firewall just aft of the very special flathead.

The resin center of this winged grille badge has been recast to say "Iskenderian 8," which is as good a nickname for this car as any.

I'm not sure if this homespun safety wire job would effectively keep the radiator mascot safe at much more than 120 mph or not, but Isky never recalls the piece flying off, so it must have been enough.

a lot about what worked and what didn't. Remember, we were still teenagers attending the colleges of hard knocks." Isky had more plans for his car, which included improved looks and attempts at more top speed.

Style or styling wasn't initially important, so he ran the car with no grille, only a radiator mounted in front of the flathead V-8; this is what it looked like when he road tripped to Mexico. He finally decided the car needed a face but didn't want to go the common routes of either a polished brass Model T grille shell or a '32 Ford shell and grille (handsome though that is). Isky wanted something totally unique for his car. So as usual he began trolling the wrecking yards for suitable grille shell options.

He recalls that, "Back then, you could buy nearly any grille shell and insert for $7 or $8." While trolling a junkyard, the

Red-painted wire wheels really show up on a black car; these Kelsey-Hayes examples were pretty robust for the time, looking sporty while still being strong enough to withstand the gaff of a hot-running flathead and countless burnouts and top-speed runs. Authentic Ford V-8 hubcaps and polished ribbed trim rings looked great in 1950 and still do today.

HOT ROD
Magazine

Ed Iskenderian in his T Roadster   JUNE, 1948   25¢

A Star Is Born: when you built a hot rod virtually from the ground up, with lots of inge-nuity and skinned knuckles along the way, there were few higher honors than your car making the cover of Hot Rod magazine and being named Hot Rod of the Month. This honor was bestowed upon the Isky T for the magazine's sixth issue, published in June 1948. (Photo Courtesy TEN: The Enthusiast Network Archive)

Hot Rod of the Month

Ed Iskenderian's T-V8 is an excellent example of craftsmanship on the part of hot rod builders. Ed not only did much of the custom work on the car's body but on the engine as well.

Iskenderian, a native Californian, was born in Tulare, moving to Los Angeles at the ripe age of one year. There he went through school, graduating from Dorsey High.

Long before leaving school, Ed began to work with cars. At 14 he did his first experimental engine work, tinkering with model T's, at that time considerably less expensive than they are today. When he was 16 he built his first hot rod, a Fronty T. After that he put together an 8 spark Multi-Flathead. (Riley equipped.)

The following year Ed decided to turn his attentions to V8's. It seemed that T cranks broke too often and too easily for the young mechanic. His first V8, however, was in a T body. In 1939 Iskenderian ran his V8 roadster at an S.C.T.A. meet on Harper Dry Lake, clocking 97 mph.

Ed built the cover car in 1940. Probably the most outstanding feature of the car is the Maxi Overheads, which Ed rebuilt to his own specifications. He made his own head covers, also filled the combustion chambers to suit the new setup. The block is '32 Ford. The roadster is running a Navarro dual manifold. Cylinders are bored to Merc. Engine is ported and relieved. Body work was done by Jimmy Summers. (Ed put on the finishing touches with a change here and there.) Also of his own design are the copper head gaskets which take

Top view of the engine shows overhead valve covers and scrolled firewall.

him two days apiece to build. The distributor is a Zephyr. (Ed did the converting.) The cam, of course, is Iskenderian. For the upholstery work, he finally had to get outside help. Laddie Jerbeck did the interior.

This car turned 120 mph at a Western Timing Association meet at El Mirage. Ed hopes to better that time in dry lakes competition in the near future. For the lakes he runs 600x16's on all four wheels. The car has a 3.78 rear end. Hydraulic brakes are a safety feature. The

attractive grill is made from the grills of two 1934 Pontiacs. (The top halves were cut off and fused together.) Steering is by Franklin. The car has Essex frame rails. Ed uses streamlined airplane struts for light brackets. The rear end suspension is '32 Ford with housing reversed (placing spring ahead of axle, lowering car a few inches).

Just one year ago Ed was married. He and his wife, Alice, are now the proud parents of a son, Roland. Right now Ed is biding his time 'til he can check Roland out in his hot rod. Mrs. Iskenderian thinks that the car is definitely not meant to be used by women with long hair. "I just finish getting all dressed up for a party, with my hair done up just so and . . . half a block's ride in the car finds my hair right back down in my face."

The car is nicknamed "La Cucaracha," a title jokingly given it in 1940 by a Mexican sheriff. The name has stuck with it ever since the Mexican trip.

Ed, a one-time cycle fan, drives his own car at dry lakes time trials. Years ago his hobby was radio building. However, he gave it up to devote all of his spare time to car building. Today Ed Iskenderian spends all of his time in automotive work. He manufactures Iskenderian custom cams in Los Angeles.

The June Hot Rod of the Month rates admiring comment wherever it goes. But, believe it or not, Ed bought the whole '24 T from which the body was made for only $4.00. That was in 1939. Just try to buy it now.

Interior has well-equipped dash with tachometer mounted in steering wheel bracket.

In 1948, magazine features weren't the multipage, splashy color spreads they are now. Being named Hot Rod of the Month earned the cover and this single-page, two-photo feature, raising Isky's and his car's status immeasurably at the time. (Photo Courtesy TEN: The Enthusiast Network Archive)

nose of a car caught his eye: an early-1930s Pontiac. He liked the shape and detailing of the grille but didn't want to run a straight-up Pontiac face on his fabulous little Ford. But the designer in his mind's eye saw the resolution of that problem by combining two top sections of this particular grille, made from two halves from two separate grilles welded together. He bought a pair of identical Pontiac grilles and shells for $15, cut each in half horizontally about halfway down, measured, matched, and welded it all together,. It yielded the unique but appropriate-looking grille and radiator shell that the car wears to this day. And it looks great.

The whole look was finished off with red-painted Kelsey-Hayes wire wheels, black lacquer paint on the $7 Model T body, and a rugged-looking saddle brown leather interior stitch job. Some early magazine reports cite the upholstery's original color as more of an oxblood maroon, but sun, time, and age have turned it a warm brown. The rear bolster was torn long ago; it literally and figuratively shows its stuffing.

The car ran well with the mildly modded 1936 flathead, and Ed ran it often and hard, including the much-storied trip to Mexico in 1939–1940, just prior to Ed's military stint. He experimented with cam, exhaust, and intake manifold/carburetor combinations, until ultimately it was run one too many times and the engine gave way and blew up. The solution was simple enough, as it wasn't too difficult or expensive to find a flathead of 1932 vintage in the junkyard, so that's what he installed. It made sense and matched up to the 1932 3-speed manual transmission he'd been running. This is the engine-transmission combo that sits in the car to this day.

The Maxi Heads

For a young guy who wanted to go fast, and clearly had his sights on a future somehow in the burgeoning speed parts business, Isky wasn't likely to be happy with a stock-configured flathead for very long. Being a curious car-crazy youth in Southern California, he'd come upon a company near downtown Los Angeles that ran and maintained fleets of trucks. Hanging around the yard, asking questions and sticking his nose under truck hoods, he was introduced to aftermarket Maxi brand "F" cylinder heads designed for the flathead Ford V-8. Conversion to these heads was intended to address two issues, the first being certain Ford V-8 heating problems because, reputedly, the exhaust valves were mounted in the engine block very close to the cylinders.

The second belief was that these heads offered the potential of increased performance for medium- to heavy-duty trucking customers. These heads are called "F" heads because they are a partial overhead valve conversion. They put only the exhaust valves into the heads that are then operated by pushrods and rocker arms; but both valves are not relocated into the heads, as would be the case in a full overhead valve conversion. This was accomplished with great success by the legendary Ardun OHV cylinder heads that came along post–World War II for these engines.

Another unusual aspect of the Maxi heads is a unique valvecover design. Instead of a single stamped-steel or cast-aluminum valvecover that runs down each bank of a V-8 engine covering the valvesprings and rocker arms of four cylinders, the Maxis split the top of the head in two, with two box-shaped valvecovers that cover two cylinders each per side. Thus the engine wears two of these little boxlike covers per cylinder bank. These unusual valvecovers resemble small metal bricks, and in a nod to style, and apart from any potential performance the head conversion may have offered, Isky comments that, "I just thought they made the engine look cool."

Mounting these heads on Ed's flathead block created at least one interesting challenge: the need to fill the old exhaust ports in the block. He didn't really want to remove the engine, so Isky reasoned that

Boys will be boys. Athan and Isky were melting lead on the stove to fill in the flathead's soon-to-be unused exhaust ports, the car was jacked up about 45-degrees so the lead could be poured into the block to settle and cool relatively level with the deck surface of the block. At the same time, the guys faked up this assuredly multi-fatal car accident scene, likely just to give their friends or parents a thrill; the "models" are Isky's brother Luther and friend Herman. (Photo Courtesy Ed Iskenderian)

This vintage Edelbrock intake runs a trio of Stromberg carbs. Isky tested a variety of intake systems on this car; he likes this one a lot, and said that his Edelbrock dual-carb "slingshot" manifold is his other favorite, both offering the best performance of everything he tried on this car.

he could jack up one side of the car about 45 degrees until the deck surface of one side of the block was relatively level, then pour molten lead into the port to fill it up.

After it cooled, he could do the same on the opposite side of the car to level out the other side of the engine, then fill the exhaust ports with lead right up to the deck surface of the block. Keep in mind that this process was only required

on the exhaust port side of each cylinder because the Maxi head's conversion only reconfigured the exhaust side of the engine to overhead valves; the intake valves remained in the block to be used. However, he did need to drill a hole in each lead plug for a pushrod to run its way up into the new head to operate the valves.

This was positively exotic stuff for the 1930s and 1940s. Unsure of the best

This is the actual four-carb manifold that Isky dreamt up, designed, and fabricated for his car in search of better breathing and more top end. As with many things that "seemed like a good idea at the time," this component was nicely made (note the artfully bent, arching fuel lines feeding off a central bullet-shaped fuel block at the center of the manifold) but didn't work as envisioned.

After testing, Isky found his car to be slower despite of all the increased carburetion, so he went back to his trusty Edelbrock "slingshot" manifold and a pair of Stromberg 97 carbs. This hand-built bit of Isky innovation sits on his desk to this day, although one of the original carbs disappeared along the way.

The car's former owner, John Athan, whom Isky calls a "gifted artist and draftsman," designed the cursive lettering, hand engraved into the specially cast aluminum valvecovers, replacing the Maxi F-heads' unusual "two box" stamped sheet-metal valvecover design. Note that the spark plugs mount at the top of the heads and that the lead for the plug on the right is missing.

This isn't the 1936 block that Isky originally bought and installed in his car. He recalled, "I blew that up somewhere along the way." But currently, and for some time, he has run a 1932 21-stud flathead; it's easy to spot the first-gen flathead Ford V-8s because of the dual water pumps mounted by the front end of each head.

way to bring adequate quantities of lead to a molten state, he borrowed pots and pans from his family's kitchen, and heated up the lead to a near boil on the kitchen stove. Isky chuckles, remembering that his mother "wasn't too crazy about that idea."

But it worked, at least for a while. Domestic lead is relatively soft and begins to soften and melt at low temperatures. So, after a few hot hard runs in the car, the home-cooked lead plugs blew out of the block, which called for revised engineering of this process. Isky opined that the newly reconfigured flathead would require lots more fuel and air than before, so he dreamt up his own intake manifold design, which he fabricated himself, using four small Stromberg carburetors.

More Experimentation

After testing the car under a variety of conditions, the manifold wasn't breathing right and wouldn't go faster than 90, so he reverted to his trusty Edelbrock "slingshot" manifold, which mounted a pair of Stromberg 48 carbs, and then the car's speed picked back up. Over time, the car has worn a Navarro intake and a different Edelbrock intake running three carbs, the latter of which is currently on the engine and has been for decades. All three solutions got the car back up to well over the 100-mph mark.

His experimentation with carbs and intakes helped the young rodders learn another lesson about carburetion. Ed recalls one time while driving up to the dry lakes, his car was running a little warm and missing and surging. He needed to feather the throttle on and off a bit to get it to run cleanly. What he didn't know was that the engine was running lean, something he never expected with multiple carburetors on his car. He asked around about the problem, and someone asked him if he still had stock jets in his carburetors.

He said, "What do you mean, stock jets?" So someone told him that by enlarging the jets a few thousandths of an inch, he could get more fuel into the engine, letting it run cooler and not "starve," as it was doing. Today he notes that "we'd never heard of such a thing; we just thought that the carburetor did its job, and if you wanted to go faster, put on a bigger carb or just add more of them! So we drilled out the carb jets about 5 thousandths of an inch, and the car ran perfect and got faster at the same time." Result!

The engine's capper is a set of custom-made aluminum valvecovers bearing the owner's last name (Iskenderian) in an elegant cursive script. Isky credits pal Athan as a "gifted artist and draftsman," so he designed and laid out the script for these one-off, personalized covers, which he then hand-carved into the metal. Cast in raw aluminum, they polish to a bright sheen but tarnish to a soft glow easily because the metal is uncoated or plated.

Because the configuration of these valvecovers wasn't the same as the "double box style" valvecovers the Maxi heads normally used, Ed fabricated a metal baseplate (or floor) to seal up the bottom of the covers and ensure they sealed tight to the heads. Regardless, these one-of-a-kind valvecovers are beautiful pieces of casting artwork and make the car and engine utterly unique to its owner/builder. The job was further finished off by a long, flow-ing, chromed dual-exhaust system that is visible from any angle of the car.

By now you may be wondering what sort of camshaft this car has run for all these decades. Funny enough, it is this car and the backstory of its cam that further opens the door to Isky entering the cam-grinding business as a profession. For a time, he ran a camshaft produced by his friend and mentor, the great Ed Winfield, but later changed it to one of his very earliest Isky Racing Cams designs. And it all worked, too.

The car's construction and finish took place over a somewhat protracted amount of time: He bought the car from Athan in the late 1930s and then got it running with the stock configuration '36 flathead V-8 prior to his trip to Mexico. Then along came World War II, which called a halt to the build for several years. The final black lacquer repaint and interior work came after the end of the war, so by the late 1940s, the Isky Roadster was looking good and standing tall, ready for an upcoming cameo on the cover of *Hot Rod* magazine.

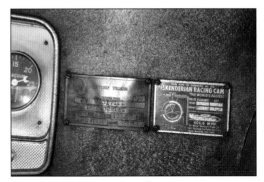

Two famous and original timing plates are affixed to the roadster's dash. The one on the left from the Western Timing Association (WTA) attesting to its 120 mph run at the El Mirage dry lakes meet on May 8, 1942. The plate on the right is Iskenderian's own timing tag, which he gave to customers who ran his cams, no matter if they ran 406.6 mph or not. The car that did was Mickey Thompson's Challenger 1 *land speed record-setting streamliner, for which Isky supplied the camshafts. A profile image of the car is represented on this tag.*

This is an early rendition of an Isky Racing Cams sticker, which of course shows a gear pattern and cam lobe in profile. John Athan designed this graphic.

Just prior to the war, he'd cranked the car up to a 111-mph top speed at Muroc, and then on May 5, 1942, at a WTA meet at El Mirage, he topped out at a more than respectable 120 mph. This event is recognized by an engraved timing plate affixed to the dashboard, then and now.

Lined up and ready to run at El Mirage. It was a good, fast, safe day for the little black car from Los Angeles, running a solid 120 mph at this WTA meet. (Photo Courtesy Ed Iskenderian Collection)

Imagine hiking your way through the back rooms of one of Isky's shops and stumbling upon this sight. One magazine writer asked Ed if they could take the car out for a drive and a few photos; he revealed that Isky insisted on grabbing a tin of old paste car wax and shining the car up before he would let it out of the building. Looks like there are many great treasures in this particular "barn." (Photo Courtesy TEN: The Enthusiast Network Archive)

So highly regarded was this fast and handsome rod that it was given the honorary title of "hot rod of the month" by the young *Hot Rod* magazine that also featured Isky's T on the cover of its June 1948 issue, and honored it with a one-page piece on page seven. It's amusing that the article's story about the how and what of the car's build differs slightly from Ed's version. The car was so strongly identified with its owner that he never gave thought of selling it, he was smart enough to just keep it. All these decades.

The Roadster Today

By the mid-1950s, he had a growing business and a growing family, so the roadster was pushed to the back of his thoughts and then actually pushed to the back of the shop, gathering more than a bit of dust, a few nicks, and some scrapes, along with quick and dirty paint touchups along the way. He no longer drove it every day, but did occasionally fire it up for a quick ride to lunch or with a friend, customer, or automotive writer in the passenger side. It was last licensed for road use in 1951, and it's only a guess when its last oil change was.

This is the much talked about, elegant, and artistic hand-cast radiator mascot that Isky bought from a friend for $2. He recalls that a half dozen or so of them were made at the time, something any hot rodder would be proud to bolt to his car, then or today. If Isky Racing Cams ever decides to launch a "nostalgia" line of hot rodding products, this should be the first item to market, and after it's digitized from the original, automated CNC machines could spin them out by the dozens or hundreds.

One particularly interesting bit of jewelry that the car wears is its unique skull-faced radiator mascot. It's obviously hand cast and comes with a backstory all its own: the look was inspired by the radiator mascot on the car of a friend of Isky and Athan. The young man (whose name Ed doesn't recall) was a handsome, very "together" guy a few years older than they, and the younger group of guys looked up to him. He may have not returned from frontline duty during World War II. Isky always liked the look of his car and particularly of this aluminum casting, and bought the original piece off his friend's car for $2.

Isky's Maxi-headed flathead is in its highly original (as in hot-rodded) state and honestly patinated. The finishes are much as they were in the early 1950s, the gas and oil stains are likely more than 50 years old, and the once–brightly polished valvecovers have dulled to a satiny aluminum finish. The whole car could stand a good clean and detail job, but to otherwise restore, repaint, or replate any of it would be a crime against hot rodding history.

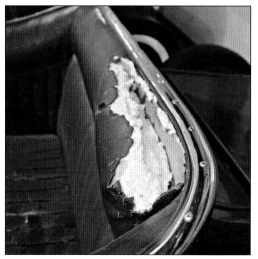

The leather is old, hard, and cracked, and is giving up a fair amount of its stuffing. It must have been a high-quality job originally, with handsome pleats and a neatly polished and fastened metal trim piece along the top of the back cushion.

Many flathead V-8s ran their distributors in the position normally occupied on later V-8s by the water pump (not a problem on this early 1932 block because it mounts its twin water pumps high on each cylinder bank, near the heads). The really hot ones dumped that low-performance system in favor of a Kong or this Scintilla Vertex magneto.

At some point, one of the headlight stanchions broke and was welded back into place. The car is unusual in that some of the welding, fab, and other workmanship is very homespun and obviously done on the run or in the middle of a long night prepping for a trip to the dry lakes, but much of the rest of the car was fabricated and finished to a high level for the time.

This angle gives you the view Isky had from the driver's side of the seat. Relatively comfy, but the T body's high seating position didn't leave a lot of room for the driver's legs between the seat cushion and the bottom of the steering wheel. The body's door openings and doors are still in place but have been welded and upholstered closed, so entry and exit are a matter of hopping up and over the bodywork. Cool!

The original paint has been touched up here, there, and most everywhere along the way. Some of the repairs are workmanlike, others are more "housepainterlike."

Isky said if he and I ever get to go out driving in this car, it'd need new tires. Ya think?

It's a little amazing that Ed Iskenderian has owned this humble little T-bucket roadster for some 80 years now. After all these years, it has enough patina to supply all the hot rods in the world. Its 60-year-old black lacquer paint is scarred and scuffed here and there and what little chrome there is has begun to bloom and tarnish. The interior leather is faded, hard, and torn in places. The old 16-inch-wide whitewalls are as dry and hard as concrete. They are worn down to cord in some places, virtually bereft of tread, and the sidewalls have shredded and yellowed from hard use and age. A couple might hold air and the rest will not.

Packing more charisma than a Cary Grant lookalike convention and more patina than the Titanic, the Isky rod is a testament to the young hot rodders who built it and raced it, and it survives with all of its many wonderful stories and inside jokes intact. Ed recalls it costing him about $1,000 (not including his own time and labor) to build, and its value now is incalculable.

A little cleaning and mechanical recommissioning would do it well, but to otherwise tear apart and redo or restore this car would be a crime of the first order. It's otherwise perfect: honest, real, and historic. It's charming, charismatic, and positively glows with hot rod history. Early hot rodding's Holy Grail? Few would argue that call.

When I began working on this book, I asked Isky two selfish questions about his fabulous, famous roadster:

"Would you ever sell it?"

"Not a chance, pal."

The Wally Parks NHRA Motorsport Museum at the Fairplex in Pomona, California, is an ideal place for the Isky rod to live out a generally quiet retirement. The museum houses many historic rods and race cars and is just a mile or so east of the Fairplex NHRA dragstrip.

"Will you take me for a ride in the car when this book is done and published?"

To which he thankfully replied, "Sure, but we'll need to put some new tires on it first."

"No problem, Ed. I'll buy them for you if I can drive."

Even as a kid, Isky liked to take pictures. This is Ed's own photograph, taken while at the wheel of his hot rod, hurtling along a then relatively vacant Jefferson Boulevard in Culver City, California. Note the carburetor stack in the foreground. This area of Los Angeles was sparsely populated at the time (1941), mostly occupied by bean fields. It grew to be the home of many wartime aerospace companies, movie studios, machine shops, the suburbanization of Los Angeles, as well as the birthplace of the speed parts industry in Southern California.

The car in front is the Ford A/V-8 of Ed's lifelong friend, John Athan. (Photo Courtesy Ed Iskenderian)

Just a few years ago, Ed and his car revisited the dry lakes for a SEMA photo shoot. Although they are both older than in the days they ran 120 mph together along the lake bed, both are looking fine and survive as great symbols of hot rod's pioneering days. (Photo Courtesy SEMA)

Even though Ed's roadster sat a fair bit as his family and business grew, he wasn't shy about taking it to the streets and blowing out the cobwebs every once in a while. The date and location aren't known for sure, but it's likely somewhere in Inglewood or Culver City, California, near Ed's shop in the late 1950s or early 1960s. The width of the street and the prevalence of new construction are clues. (Photo Courtesy TEN: The Enthusiast Network Archive)

Chapter 3

$100 A DAY

Isky never was much of a biker guy but must have borrowed one to get around Los Angeles when he was home on leave during his time in the Army Air Corps. The significant thing about this photo isn't the motorcycle, or particularly Ed in uniform, it's the only photo Isky could find of John Athan's Mercury Tool and Die shop. The back room was where he opened his business with one machine, producing one product (camshafts for the flathead Ford V-8) and one employee: himself. (Photo Courtesy Ed Iskenderian)

World War II was over and Ed finished his military stint. He was now back home in Los Angeles and contemplating his working future. Between playing with cars, learning from older guys who built and raced cars, and, most particularly, mentoring with Ed Winfield, young Iskenderian decided that he had some ideas and that the need and demand was enough that he'd try his hand at producing high-performance and racing camshafts.

An Idea for a Career Is Formed

"I bought my first cam from Winfield," Isky notes. "And he mentored me in so many ways, which he didn't have to do. Even though I later picked up the nickname of 'The Camfather,' Ed Winfield is really the forefather of the modern performance camshaft industry; absolutely the old master."

As noted, Ed Winfield had coached the young Isky how to modify a cylindrical grinding machine into a cam grinder, so just after the war Ed purchased a used sur-

plus 1930s-era Norton grinding machine for $600. He pruned off all the unneeded bits and made the additions and modifications necessary to set it up with the "rocking bar" attachment necessary to make camshafts.

Nicknames such as "Isky Racing Cams" and "The Camfather" came some years later, but he initially hung his shingle as Ed Iskenderian Racing Cams. It was just Ed and his big grinding machine, so he didn't need much space to start out with, but he did need "three-phase" electrical service to power the equipment.

As with many things in his life, he cooked up an answer to this question with his pal John Athan. Athan owned and operated Mercury Tool and Die Company in nearby Culver City and had an empty back room at the shop. It wasn't a huge space, and the floor was dirt, but it had the heavy-duty electrical service Ed needed to operate his equipment. Plus, it was close to home and his landlord was his best pal, so it was an easy and logical solution.

Ed felt he could really improve the performance of Ford's venerable flathead V-8.

This particularly handsome flathead build up is more recent; it uses Edelbrock heads and a pair of Ford carburetors on an Offenhauser intake manifold. This nicely detailed flatty sits under the hood of a fine '40 Ford Deluxe.

"It's really a very good design, with a lightweight valvetrain (just a tappet, the valve, a spring, and a retainer, but no pushrods or rocker arms)" if not the world's most efficient breathing, but the factory originally engineered it with pretty modest performance (stock versions in the 1940s put out around 100 hp at best, which was impressive for a low-cost production street automobile) with a camshaft profile that was configured for smooth and quiet running, a good idle, reasonable low-end torque, and fuel economy.

Iskenderian's idea was what he called a "fast action" cam that opened the intake valves earlier and much more aggressively, held them open longer (more duration), and closed them later and quicker than the factory cam. This is what he set out, initially, to produce at his new "factory." "The stock cam had 'clearance ramps' designed to take up some existing slack prior to opening the valves, and also in the name of quieter running, so I did away with those in my design."

A Bit of 404 Mystery

You will recall that in the Foreword, Vic Edelbrock tells the story of his father, Vic Sr., having an idea for a somewhat radical flathead cam profile, and then taking it to Ed to have it ground onto a cam so he could test and evaluate it.

Ed tells a different story for the inspiration of what would become his famous 404 Ford flathead cam. Isky maintains that he'd been asked to do some repair work on an Offenhauser midget racer engine. While analyzing this racing-only engine, he

Isky's ultimate flathead cam came to be known as the 404 that Ed originally priced at $30 each. They're up to $110 in this 1952 advertisement, which demonstrates the new cam's power curve on a graph and calls out the name of earlier flathead grinds. (Photo Courtesy Ed Iskenderian)

This hardworking group of young hot rodders is Bonneville-bound, as they leave Riverside, California. The two hot rods at left had to do at least double duty as a competition car and a luggage and parts wagon. Note the triple-carb intake set up in the hand of the young man at left.

Many great racing drivers and car builders began their competitive wrenching and steering-wheel turning days as hot rodders. Pay particular attention to the guy wearing the tall cat-in-the-hat on the right with the big smile and his hand in the air. Dirty T-shirt and '34 Ford coupe notwithstanding, he's none other than the All American Racer Dan Gurney. From humble beginnings comes great speed. (Photo Courtesy Gurney Family Archives, Roma Gurney)

When Vic Edelbrock was casting about for cam grinders who could design and produce a hot, high-RPM cam for the new small-block Chevy V-8, Isky was among them. His profile design was the only cam that met the criteria for increased horsepower and the ability to run high RPM. This is Vic Edelbrock Sr. dyno testing an Edelbrock-modified small-block with an impressive six-carb intake system. (Photo Courtesy Edelbrock LLC)

was impressed with its cam profiles, even though it was a very different configuration. The flathead V-8 was a valve-in-block and cam-in-block 8-cylinder, while the exotic Offy was only four cylinders with double overhead camshafts.

Ed says that the Offy cam profiles inspired his ultimate design for the flathead, with no mention of Edelbrock Sr. coming to him with a cam profile in his head. Each man stands by his story, and unless they get together and mentally duke it out as to who is really right, this remains somewhat of an unanswered question, but actually of little consequence.

Not really knowing how much money he could expect to make, Ed timed how long it took him to produce a finished camshaft, and then judged the hours in a day he reasonably expected to work at the machine. He believed he could produce up to five finished camshafts per day, and by selling them to dealers, speed shops, and racers at a wholesale cost of $20 each, that meant he could theoretically gross $100 per day of combined labor and product.

His costs were relatively minimal: his time, overhead, machine maintenance, and the cost of the specially alloyed 4-inch steel bar stock that became each cam. He could machine his design on a used but still serviceable stock Ford camshaft, finding his high-performance profile "within" the lobe of the stock cam; these used pieces cost him $2 each to buy as raw material. If the customer, such as later NASCAR racers, insisted on the cam being machined from new metal stock, that "blank" cost him $7. He set the retail price of each cam at $30 (his cost per piece was about $20, given the cost of materials and his machine work time), giving those same speed shops, dealers, and wholesalers the chance to make $10 per cam sold. And he felt he could live well on $100 per day of production.

So he went to work, on that single used grinding machine, making high-performance cams for the still popular and viable flathead Ford V-8. This was 1946, and Ed was 25 years old. He remem-

bers feeling like he "bluffed" his way into the business, with some people turning him away, saying, "You're still a kid, how could you know much about building racing cams?"

Iskenderian recognizes the development and launch of a variety of important engines as turning points for the growth of his company. It all began with the flathead Ford V-8. In 1949, Oldsmobile and Cadillac each launched new and technically advanced overhead valve V-8 engines.

A Star Is Born

For 1955, Chevrolet changed the engine world with the launch of the new "small-block Chevrolet V-8." It became a game changer because it proved to be highly versatile for production car and truck use, easily adapted to high-performance street machines, and then ultimately racing and marine uses. It is an overall great engine that responds to the hop-up treatment and loves to make horsepower.

The seminal "small-block Chevy" has been produced and sold all over the world in a variety of displacements and performance levels for more than 60 years. Ford's new "Y-block" overhead valve V-8 was introduced a year prior to the small-block Chevy, and although it is not as innately good and versatile as the competing Chevy engine, the Y-block brought the curtain down on the venerable flathead, which was produced from 1932 through the 1953 model year.

Chrysler got its licks in with a variety of overhead valve V-8s, including the vaunted "Hemi" with its unique hemispherical combustion chamber design, introduced in 1951. Ed also recognizes the 1960s Ford small-block "Fairlane" V-8, which has powered Indy winners, Le Mans winners, the first Shelby Cobras, and millions of Mustangs. And, of course, Chrysler's legendary "street Hemi" of the mid-1960s, the birth of the big-block Chevrolet, and finally a substantial redevelopment of the original

Isky acknowledges Karl Orr as one of the first speed shop owners to take a chance on a young, unknown cam grinder new to the business. Veda and Karl Orr were quite the competitors at the dry lakes. Karl ran the dusty colored '32 roadster and Mrs. Orr (one of the few record-holding women to run the lakes) ran the shinier, fully restored '32 in the background.

One of Karl Orr's previous Model A racers ran a 4-cylinder Ford engine, with a host of upgrades, modifications, and an Ed Winfield cam; he is quoted as being none too happy with it. It mattered little, because he ultimately upgraded to this handsome Deuce highboy with a V-8.

Vedo Orr took her first run at the dry lakes after a little goading by her husband; she liked it, she did well, and she ended up being the best-known female dry lakes competitor at the time. She ultimately built her own car and competed against her husband, Karl.

Mrs. Orr had a way with words, for a time publishing a small newsletter keeping SCTA members connected and updated when several of the guys went off to war. She ultimately wrote and published her own Hot Rod Pictorial magazine, which was first published in 1949 by Floyd Clymer.

Ed Iskenderian and his car are pictured in this magazine, which has since been republished by and is now available from Veloce Press. (Photo Courtesy Veloce Press)

Isky and the C-T Automotive boys ham it up a bit with this ancient mill wheel they must have found in the desert; that's Isky pretending to grind a cam with it. Note the team lettering on the side of the truck, and the fact that all of these gents are wearing Iskenderian Racing Cams T-shirts. (Photo Courtesy TEN: The Enthusiast Network Archive)

small-block Chevy V-8 in 1997, called the LS1 (which has since led to several more larger and more powerful small-blocks in the LS series).

That's not to say that any other engine not mentioned here isn't significant, but it's these major players that each represented growth opportunities and fertile expansion ground for a company such as Iskenderian's.

Ed's original flathead V-8 cam ultimately performed as promised after some development work. It had one potential downside for street use, in that it was noisy. It was opening up the intake valves so aggressively that Ed said he could hear an Isky cam–equipped flathead-powered car coming from blocks away, those aggressive "fast action" high-lift cam lobes really smacking the valves open. But it helped the little V-8 rev and perform. And soon his one-man, one-machine crew couldn't keep up with increasing demand, so Ed added another employee, machinist Norris Baronian, who would "rough in" four or five cams a day, doing the basic lobe grinding, and then leaving it to Ed to do the final finish work on each piece.

Ed particularly recognizes the two speed shops that really supported his early efforts by buying and stocking his wares, Louis Senter and Jack Anders, who owned and operated Ansen Automotive.

Fellow dry lakes competitor Karl Orr had his own shop and sold a lot of Ed's cams. Ed had an unusual way of opening up new sales territories; if a customer called up from an area that didn't have a shop or dealer carrying Iskenderian Cams, and if Ed liked the person's attitude and demeanor, he might offer that customer the chance to become an Isky dealer for his locale. Sometimes these were small, backyard racer types that would only sell a few cams a year. Ed remembers one particular small dealer that didn't have a warehouse or storefront; Ed paid a visit to his home one time and asked how he marketed Isky cams. The man lifted up his bed; his stock of new cams and accessories was neatly stored there. Some distributors' "dealerships" were the beds of their pickup trucks.

Tracking every bit of growth and new product over Isky Racing Cams 70-plus-year history would be somewhat tedious, but suffice it to say that Iskenderian and his growing band of engineers, hot rodders, craftsmen, draftsmen, and machinists worked hard innovating new products when it came to camshaft designs and better performing valvetrain components. Much of the company's growth and success came from its own ingenuity and willingness to experiment and innovate, plus customer demand

This is Isky's first Hot Rod *magazine ad. It invites the reader or potential customer to write for more detailed information on how this cam performed. (Photo Courtesy Ed Iskenderian)*

and the effectiveness of Isky's marketing and promotional efforts. And there were external factors that moved the company forward; many of them in the form of the new, performance-oriented engines (noted above) that came to market in new cars.

Another important external force was the maturation of some of the major forms of American motorsport. The birth, or more correctly, the organization or formalization of top speed or "land speed record" racing at the Bonneville Salt Flats in Utah in the early 1950s supplanted most of the former "dry lakes" competition held by the local car clubs in the 1930s, later 1940s, and early 1950s. Another reason that dry lakes racing was heading toward extinction is that most of the land belonged to the United States government, and over time much of it was annexed to expand the borders of ever-growing Air Force bases.

The other major change was the professionalization of quarter-mile drag racing with the birth of the National Hot Rod Association in 1951. Another was certainly the birth of a professional stock car racing series, which we now know as NASCAR, in February 1948.

After Isky was in business for a little while in the early 1950s, he wasn't always

sure where his cams were going, who was using them, or even how. He was very pleased one day when he heard from a NASCAR racing team from the Carolinas. He doesn't remember who it was, but they ran his cams, really liked the performance, and wanted to buy more.

One of the advantages of his "fast action" flathead cams was a smooth, strong, mid-range torque curve, which allowed the cars to power strongly out of the sweeping curves on the oval tracks. He recalls that the NASCAR racers wanted their cams ground on brand-new cam core blanks. He shipped the cam to the Carolinas via airmail, which, at the time, was a semi-exotic and expensive way to ship parcels. A special race-only "mushroom" version of his flathead cam was created for use primarily in Mercury engines, used in the "modified stock car" class.

The Influence of Petersen Publishing Company

Ed instinctively believed in the value of advertising and the power of promotion. He was excited to see the launch of a new magazine called *Hot Rod*, published by hot rodder and photographer Robert E. Petersen and finance man Robert Lindsay in January 1948. But he was disappointed that he didn't hear about it prior to its launch so that he could have bought an ad in the first issue. Even though his company not appearing in that first issue was spilt milk, Iskenderian acted quickly to make sure he had an ad in the second. He contacted Petersen and signed up for an advertising schedule in *Hot Rod*, which cost $10 per column inch: $30 for a one-column-wide by 3-inch-tall ad and $20 for a one-column-wide by 2-inch-tall ad.

He remembers the young, handsome Petersen coming to his home or shop to collect the $20 or $30 (cash or check) each time they put out a new issue. Isky chuckles at the notion of Petersen selling his own ad placements and doing his own collections; from these humble beginnings he built the Petersen Publishing Company, publisher of dozens of specialty enthusiast titles for a variety of genres, including automotive, racing, several motorcycle magazines, gun and hunting magazines, plus women's and young girls' titles. This should be no surprise; he was married only once, to model and frequent race queen Margie McNally. She strongly supported the growth and maturation of young women and oversaw the titles aimed at female readers. Prior to their passing, the Petersens sold their company for nearly half a billion dollars. From humble beginnings . . .

Ed recalls that in the earliest days of his company when he first began running his magazine advertisements, the normal means of communication was via letter. There was, of course, no Internet or e-mail, and long distance calls across the country were expensive, whereas a letter and a stamp only cost a few cents. He was pleasantly surprised when he began getting letters from racers and hot rodders around the country asking questions about his products, or wanting other technical advice. Sometimes the letter contained a check or a postal money order with an order for parts.

Ed felt that for a fledgling business such as his, he needed to demonstrate clear interest in the writer's questions at least equal to that of their interest in his products, so he answered every letter, one by one. Ed didn't know how to type, and he didn't have an office staff or secretary, so he hired a local college student who could type to help him respond to his mail. Sometimes it was a letter a week, sometimes a dozen, usually heaviest when a new issue of *Hot Rod* hit the stands and someone new saw his ads. Ed used to dictate his replies, one by one, while his young "temp" typed out the reply letter. At the end of each day his typist sealed up and mailed the letters. So, in the early days, Ed Iskenderian even managed his own customer service department.

Over time, Isky Racing Cams has advertised in a wide variety of automo-tive enthusiast publications, but always remained loyal to *Hot Rod* because Ed felt it spoke directly to his customer base. It wasn't long before Isky was running full-page advertisements in *Hot Rod* just like "big grown-up car companies."

One of Ed's more challenging promotional exercises came in 1950, when a group of hot rodders and racers (Petersen and Lindsay among them) elected to host a major hot rod show at the Los Angeles National Guard Armory. The show had actually begun in 1948, so the 1950 event was the third edition of it.

The promoters were scouring Los Angeles for the best hot rods and racing cars to fill the show and encouraged Iskenderian to rent booth space at the show to expose and promote his business. He immediately loved the idea and wanted to have some promotional materials to hand out to attendees and potential customers, so they'd remember his company and its products. He had some photographs, a logo, some ideas for copy, and illustrations of his various products, but not the skill to design and publish such a brochure or catalog.

Less than three days before the opening of the show, a young man named Leon Cook knocked on Ed's door, looking for work. He presented himself as a graphic artist, and Ed asked if he could produce a brochure for an upcoming trade show. Cook said he could, but then Isky cautioned him that the show was three days away. He said he could do it, and the results are seen here. It ended up being Isky Racing Cams' first catalog, copyright dated 1950, with a price per copy of 25 cents.

Most of the graphics and the photos were reproduced in black ink on off-white card stock, with red as an accent color. Ed is very proud of this piece, describing it as "state-of-the-art literature in the racing cam industry" for the time. It was the first of decades of catalogs his business produced. The back page showed photos of several event and championship winning cars (and one boat) that ran Isky Cams, plus a testimonial letter from noted sports

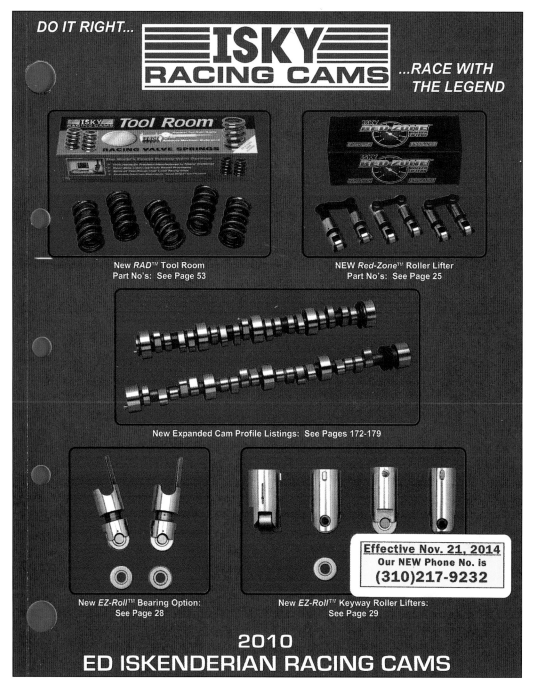

Ring-punched parts catalogs are as old as speed parts and speed shops themselves. This is, to date, the most recent paper catalog Isky has printed. Everything in it is available on the Internet now, and can be downloaded for free and updated as the company introduces new products. (Photo Courtesy Ed Iskenderian)

The back cover of Isky's 2010 catalog lists some of the imaginative names under which its various equipment is produced and marketed. These catalogs are hundreds of pages and are jammed with many pages of technical, installation, and setup information. The first one cost a quarter, and then they were a dollar for quite some time. This final printing is still a bargain at five bucks. (Photo Courtesy Ed Iskenderian)

This is an amazing period photo of the Ansen Automotive Isky Racing Cams booth at the 1950 Los Angeles Armory hot rod show. Isky is the young man on the right, wearing a suit and tie and his trademark mop of black hair. (Ed does not recall the names of the other two men in the photo.)

Note the radical double-overhead camshaft flathead V-8 at the lower left; pretty exotic stuff for a flathead in 1950. Ed recalls that it was developed for Southern California car dealer and racing team owner Bob Estes, who ran cars and teams at Indianapolis and Bonneville. If this engine was ever a runner, and still exists somewhere, it would be a highly prized by vintage hot rodders and racers, and likely worth a fortune. (Photo Courtesy Ed Iskenderian)

car team owner and racer Miles Collier. He thanked Ed for his products' contribution to the Mercury V-8 that powered the Riley that won the Sports Car Grand Prix of Watkins Glen, New York.

This brochure was produced long before the days of computerized layout machines and software, and long before digital printing. The entire eight-page piece was produced and laid out by hand, and offset printed in just three days.

Ed's company was small and just a few years in business at the time, but he was keenly aware of innovative ways to get the word out about his products. It also proved to be a harbinger of things to come for Isky Racing Cams; Isky's informative catalogs became one of the company's trademarks. Every year, from

the mid-1950s through 2010, Isky Racing Cams published a detailed catalog of all its products, well over 200 pages at the time the latest book-form edition was produced, although it's all available now on the Internet in web page or downloadable PDF catalog form.

Put It in Writing

Ed also believed strongly that company catalogs and advertisements should educate and inform the customer, as well as promote and sell products. Isky's catalogs are rich in technical material and advice, helping the customer select the right camshaft, springs, or other related products, and include detailed installation guides on how to set up the engine with

Cam of Records and Successes....

ISKENDERIAN

RACING CAMS

1950 Catalogue

Twenty-Five Cents

Copyright 1960

Printed in U.S.A.

This is Iskenderian Racing Cam's first brochure and catalog, produced in just a couple of days in all its eight-page two-color glory, packing a lot of information and photos for a quarter. (Photo Courtesy Ed Iskenderian)

Special Mushroom Track Grinds

Qualities

The mushroom track grind is truly the last word in cams for the large bore and stroked Mercury's. Ground on the 21-A 1948 Mercury Iron Cam and using 8 special 3/16" base Mushroom Lifters; a lift of .375" is made possible on the intakes. In conjunction with this high lift, a high rate of acceleration is used producing a superior valve opening diagram which would be impossible to obtain on the standard 1" followers.

Dynamometer Test

In October of 1949, we ran the Mushroom Cam in a 3 5/16 bore, 4 1/8 stroke Mercury engine on the Eddlebrock Dynamometer. After 2 hours of low speed running to loosen up the new engine a full throttle run was made producing a peak horsepower of 211 at 5100 R.P.M. along with the highly desirable characteristic of a nearly flat horsepower curve between 3500 and 5500 R.P.M. Below are a few horse-power readings at various revs.

```
4000——194 H.P.
4500——205  ''
5000——210  ''
5300——206  ''
```

We contend that any good mechanic can duplicate these results with the use of the Mushroom Cam #1023.

Equipment Used in Mushroom Engine

The following equipment was used: 8½ to 1 heads, 3 carburetors manifold, 48 Stromberg carburetors on straight methanol with 82 main jets. The engine had a mild port job. 3/16 relieve at the bore out to the gasket, stock valves with 30 degree seats on the intakes only, and cut-away underneath for a maximum flow and 20 degree ignition advance.

Recent Successes

Most recent success was when Harry Hull, well known for his engine building of Woodbury, Conn., installed the No. 1023 near the close of the 1949 season for the championship races, he won the last 2-100 lap feature races and took 2nd in the 50-lap feature run by United Stock Car Racing Association of New York State, racing against the fastest cars on the east coat.

Mercury Mushroom Cam Prices

Mushroom V8 Track Grind #1023 complete with
8 Mushroom Tappets $80.00

NOTE: The spot facing tool shown in sketch is sent with the purchase of the Mushroom Track Grind at an additional cost of $12.00. When spot facer is returned postpaid within 30 days the $12.00 deposit is refunded.

Buick Valve Spring Adapters
For Intakes Only — 16 per set ....only $8.00
(For High R.P.M. Applications Only)

TOP CENTER
23° | 18°
68° | 62°
BOTTOM CENTER

LIFT
IN. .375
EX. .345

V8-60 Mushroom Track Grind #620

This cam has the same characteristics as our Mercury Mushroom cam.

V8-60 Mushroom Track Grind #620. Complete with
8 Special Mushroom Tappets $80.00

NOTE: Spot facing tool rental charge also $12.00.

TOP CENTER
18° | 15°
57° | 64°
BOTTOM CENTER

LIFT
IN. .300
EX. .270

V8-60 Stock Tappet Grinds

#600 Recommended for variable conditions, dirt or asphalt tracks and marine use.

Used by the famous MEN SING BROS. midget in winning the 1949 Iowa championship.

New #600 Outright $40.00
Grinding price 30.00

#601 Recommended for longer or slick tracks and marine straight-away racing.

Used by Art Jacobson of Omaha, Nebraska, in his powerful No. 44 to win Iowa High Point Standing.

New #601 — Outright $43.00
Grinding price 33.00

Racing V8-60 Valve Springs—
Wound extra long from long life Swedish Steel Spring wire—20 lbs. greater tension without spacer......$4.00 set
Needed on ALL our V8-60 Track Grinds

NOTE—New Timing Gear included **FREE** on outright V8-60 Cam Purchases

---

V8 Cam Grinds Offered

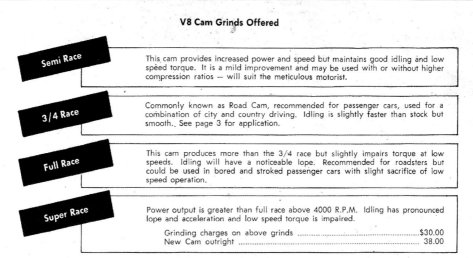

Semi Race — This cam provides increased power and speed but maintains good idling and low speed torque. It is a mild improvement and may be used with or without higher compression ratios -- will suit the meticulous motorist.

3/4 Race — Commonly known as Road Cam, recommended for passenger cars, used for a combination of city and country driving. Idling is slightly faster than stock but smooth. See page 3 for application.

Full Race — This cam produces more than the 3/4 race but slightly impairs torque at low speeds. Idling will have a noticeable lope. Recommended for roadsters but could be used in bored and stroked passenger cars with slight sacrifice of low speed operation.

Super Race — Power output is greater than full race above 4000 R.P.M. Idling has pronounced lope and acceleration and low speed torque is impaired.

Grinding charges on above grinds $30.00
New Cam outright 38.00

V8 Track Grinds

We pioneered these track grinds and use a HIGH RATE of acceleration whereby long duration and overlap can be reduced. They are famous for their terrific low speed torque with ability to outperform the Super Race cam in the higher R.P.M. bracket. These cams make maximum use of the stock 1" tappets and are being used by the fastest midgets, roadsters and modified stock cars in the country.

V8 Track Grind No. 1007

This cam was used in winning the 1949 New York Stock Car Championship. Recommended for roadsters and stock cars on short tracks. Standard displacement Mercurys in many cases when equipped with this camshaft are able to out-perform large bored and stroked Mercurys.

V8 Track Grind No. 1014

This cam has slightly more duration on the intakes than the No. 1007 and is recommended for the longer race tracks in moderate displacement Mercurys.

V8 Track Grind No. 1015-B

This cam is of higher lift and recommended for the large bored and stroked Mercurys on any size track. Used by Red Cummings in winning New England modified stock car championship for 1949 in the famous Litwin "Dynamite Special".

Grinding Charges on Track Grinds ..... **No. 1007, No. 1014, No. 1015-B** $40.00

New Cam outright 48.00

Cam Accessories

Adjustable Tappets V8 Ford and Mercury, per set.............$13.60
Valve Springs—Lincoln Zephyr
   Necessary wtih all Ford & Mercury V-8 Cams, per set...... 4.00
Streamlined Intake Valves V8. Ground under head as shown in sketch to allow for maximum flow and consequent increased volumetric efficiency, with 30 degree seat.
   Ford & Mercury V8, 1932-50 and V8-60 (specify), ea.......$1.25
   New Guides machined as shown in sketch, ea.................. .50

Grinding Charges

Most Other Cars—Semi, 3/4 or full race

4 Cylinder Auto Cams $35.00
6 Cylinder Auto Cams 40.00
8 Cylinder Auto Cams 50.00
12 Cylinder Auto Cams 50.00

Track Grind. $5.00 extra

SHIPPING INSTRUCTIONS

When sending cams in for regrinding, ship via Railway Express or Parcel Post.

"Do not send by Bus Line.", All prices F.O.B. Los Angeles, California. 50% deposit required on C.O.D. orders.

5% Excise Tax on Outright or Exchange Cam Purchases. No Tax on Regrinding Customer's Cam.

Whenever possible always patronize your nearest dealer.

FAST FORD OR MERCURY V-8 ROAD CAR

Compression Ratio

No single engine modification will increase power as easily and quickly as raising the compression ratio. It is possible to mill the stock heads a maximum of .050" without necessity of redoming to clear the pistons. This raises compression ratio to approximately 7 to 1. However, manufactured Aluminum Racing Heads are recommended because of the improved combustion chamber design, and the fact that Aluminum having a higher rate of heat conductivity enables the use of higher compression ratios of 8½ to 8¾ to 1 on premium ethyl gasoline.

Racing Cam

We recommend our 3/4 racing camshaft for all around city and country driving. This cam is highly developed and with its moderately improved valve opening diagram produces silent operation, good idling, acceleration and fairly good top speed. Higher tension Lincoln Zephyr Valve Springs are required and adjustable Tappets recommended for convenience of installation.

Dual Intake Manifold

With the higher compression ratio and racing camshaft there becomes a heavy draw upon the single carburetor causing the mixture to become lean. Larger jets could be installed in the single carburetor to correct the mixture ratio but this does not come near satisfying the demand. Consequently, dual carburetion becomes essential to eliminate the last remaining restriction or choke in the induction system.

Fuel Economy and Durability

If the above engine is driven conservatively, accelerating gradually, and cruising at speeds of 40 to 50 miles per hour, an increase of 2 miles mileage per gallon is quite feasable due to the gain in Thermal efficiency obtained with the higher compression ratios. Contrary to common belief, high compression ratios are not severe on connecting rod bearings. The greatest load to the connecting rods is due to high RPM. If care is taken not to over rev the engine in low and 2nd gears, one could expect practically the same durability as a stock engine.

Further increase in power output could be obtained from the above engine by overboring, long stroking, intake port enlargement, etc. However we have endeavored to list the most important modifications to suit the average motorist's pocketbook.

SUMMARY

We have now increased the power output in 3 ways:

1. With the dual carburetion we have not only increased the supply of fuel and air to each valve port but have distributed it more evenly.
2. The 3/4 racing camshaft with longer opening periods and higher valve lift allows a greater amount of fuel and air charge to enter the cylinders.
3. Finally, the charge after entering the cylinders is compressed to a higher degree producing greater power and efficiency.

HOT CHEVROLET ROAD CAR

The following modifications are recommended for a fast and practical Chevrolet Passenger car Engine for City and Hi-way use:

Compression Ratio

Cylinder heads on the 1941 and later models can be milled .100" to .150". After milling the intake valve seats must be sunk (spot faced) at least the same amount that has been milled from the surface of the head. If this is not done the intake valves will strike the pistons. In spot facing the intake valve seats, care must be taken to select a cutter of at least 1 7/8" in diameter so as not to cause the intake valves to become masked. After the intake valves have been put in place a straight edge passed over the surface of the head should clear the intake valve heads by .010".

On the earlier heads, 1937 to 1940 inclusive .060" is the maximum that can be milled off without the dome pistons striking the head. If head is redomed (which takes a special cutter) and intake valve seats recessed, more can be milled from these heads. However, it should be pointed out that a 60 thousandths mill on these early heads gives the same increase in compression ratio as .100" milled from the late heads due to the difference in combustion chamber design.

G.M.C. Stellite (Group 1) exhaust valves should be used since they resist burning. Care should also be taken to see that the exhaust valve seats are at least .125" wide, which also aids in cooling the valves.

3/4 Racing Camshaft

The 3/4 racing camshaft gives an increase of nearly .060" lift at the valves, along with an improved valve opening diagram. Idling will be slightly faster than stock, torque or lugging ability and top speed is good.

Dual Carburetion

A dual Chevrolet Manifold is necessary as with the higher compression ratio and 3/4 race cam there is a demand for additional fuel and air as well as balanced distribution. Either dual Carters, 1950 Rochesters or Stromberg Replacement Carburetors may be used. The Strombergs being preferable and the Rochesters as second choice.

Performance

The above engine properly set-up will give a Chevrolet greatly increased acceleration and a top speed of approximately 100 M.P.H. without any other changes. Premium Ethyl must be used to obtain maximum benefit and even with 3 or 4 degrees of additional spark advance over stock pinging is not evident. If the car is driven conservatively pressing the throttle gradually when accelerating and cruising at 40 to 50 miles per hour, 1 to 2 miles per gallon on increased mileage is obtained due to increased efficiency.

SERVICE OFFERED

For those not equipped to work over the Chevrolet head, we offer the following service:—Ship your head in by Truck Lines or Railway express less the Rocker Arms but with valves and springs in place. We will mill, spot face intake seats, reface intake valves, regrind intake and exhaust seats, install new G.M.C. exhaust valves, slightly increase tension on valve springs, assemble and ship back ready to install within 10 days at a charge of $60.00 C.O.D.

Eddlebrock Chevrolet dual manifold with complete throttle linkage, fittings, and instructions $42.50

3/4 race camshaft .... $35.00 exchange
$45.00 outright

VALVE TIMING FOR MAXIMUM OUPUT

The Stock Car Camshaft

The camshaft design of the American Passenger Car Engine stresses slow speed performance and smooth idling. To bring out these characteristics 5 to 10% of the horsepower is sacrificed. This output can be increased from 20 to as high as 100% with the use of our reground racing camshafts teamed with higher compression ratios and multi-carburetion.

Basic Cam Design

The ideal cam would open the intake valve instantly to full lift at approximately top dead center, dwell in the full open position until approximately 40 degrees after bottom center and then close instantly. Naturally, such abrupt action would create terrific mechanical stress and many other complications. Consequently cams must be contoured to open and close the valves in a more gentle manner.

Overlap

It is now understood that in actuating the valves we are limited to certain rates of valve acceleration and deceleration. Since it is necessary that we maintain a reasonable amount of valve lift over the greater portion of the intake and exhaust strokes we have no alternative but to lead and lag the valve opening periods to such an extent that the intake and exhaust cycles actually overlap. From first glance this valve overlap would seem rather detrimental, which it is at slow speeds. However, at higher engine speeds this deficiency diminishes and becomes a slight asset, as explained later on under "Exhaust Closes".

Intake Opens

In the timing diagram one notes that the intake valve begins opening 20 degrees before top dead center or before the piston starts on the suction stroke. This is done to give the valve a head start on the piston and we find that at top center the valve will be well off its seat, so as to offer little resistance to the incoming charge.

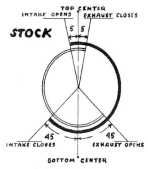

Intake Closes

Now note that the intake valve remains opened some 64 degrees after bottom center which is long after the piston has changed direction and is coming up on the compression stroke. This is best explained by the fact that the intake charge having been in motion builds up kinetic energy and tends to continue to flow long after the piston changes direction, should the intake valve have been closed at bottom center here would be a considerable throttling effect on the intake charge.

Exhaust Opens

Looking at the exhaust valve, it is seen that the valve begins opening some 64 degrees before bottom center or before the power stroke has actually been completed. This slight loss of useful power is offset by the fact that the hot exhaust gasses leave the cylinder partially under their own pressure, thereby reducing the effort on the engines part to expel the burnt gasses on the upward stroke of the piston.

Exhaust Closes

Notice that the exhaust valve remains open for some time after top center, here again kinetic energy comes into play in that the burnt gases continue to flow out and scavenge the cylinder. It might be added that on some inclined overhead valve engines when definite diameter and length of exhaust stacks are used a mild super charge is effected by the exhaust gasses. Actually drawing the intake charge in during the short overlap period.

The Valve Opening Diagram

From the foregoing it is obvious that it is of no use to compare the cam designs with respect only to actual points of valve opening and closing. The important factors are lift and rate of lift and only when a graph is drawn by plotting valve lift with respect to crankshaft rotation can a good study be made. The necessary tools are a .375" minimum range dial test indicator to read valve lift in thousandths of an inch and a timing disk to be attached to the crankshaft. Valve Lift is then checked every 5 degrees of crank rotation and recorded on graph paper giving the valve opening diagram.

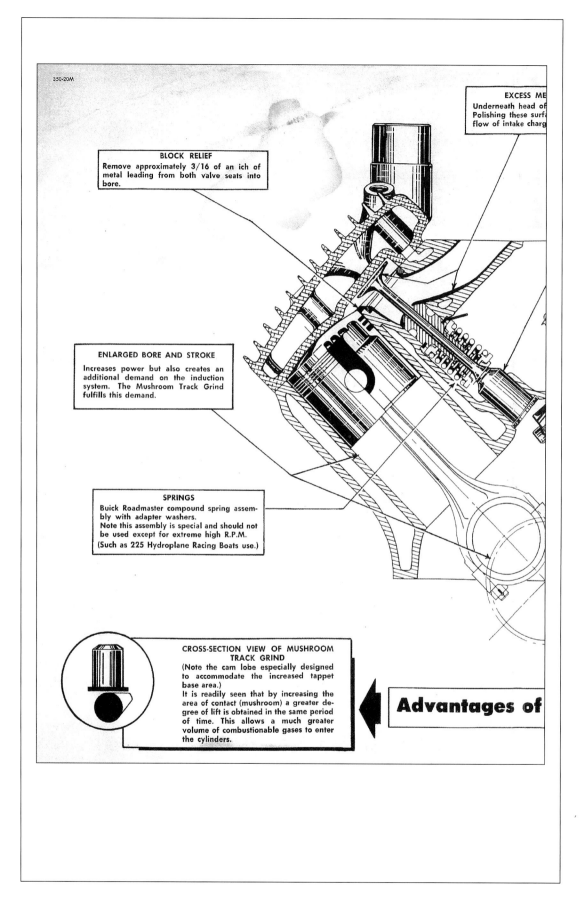

BLOCK RELIEF
Remove approximately 3/16 of an ich of metal leading from both valve seats into bore.

EXCESS ME
Underneath head of Polishing these surf flow of intake charg

ENLARGED BORE AND STROKE
Increases power but also creates an additional demand on the induction system. The Mushroom Track Grind fulfills this demand.

SPRINGS
Buick Roadmaster compound spring assembly with adapter washers.
Note this assembly is special and should not be used except for extreme high R.P.M.
(Such as 225 Hydroplane Racing Boats use.)

CROSS-SECTION VIEW OF MUSHROOM TRACK GRIND
(Note the cam lobe especially designed to accommodate the increased tappet base area.)
It is readily seen that by increasing the area of contact (mushroom) a greater degree of lift is obtained in the same period of time. This allows a much greater volume of combustionable gases to enter the cylinders.

Advantages of

350-20M

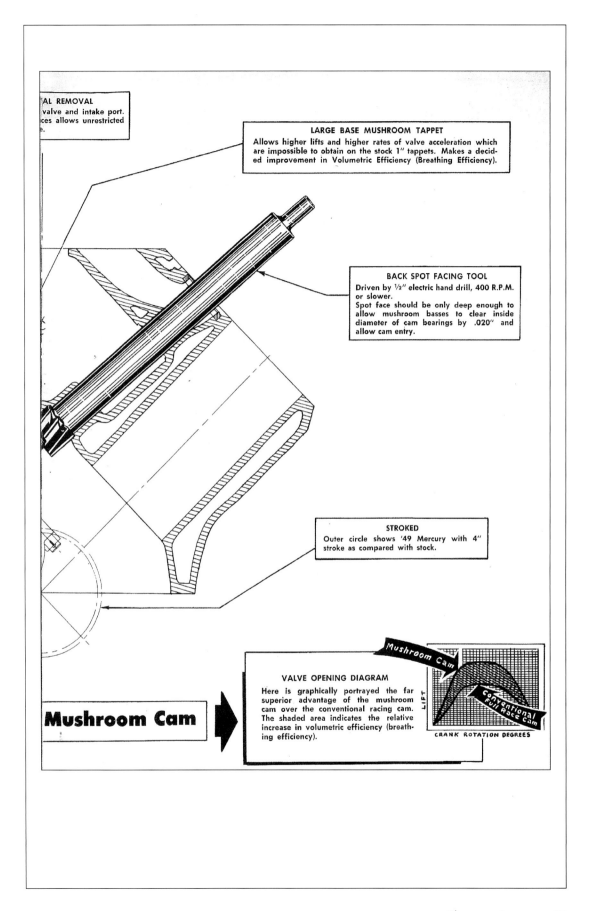

AL REMOVAL
valve and intake port.
ces allows unrestricted
e.

LARGE BASE MUSHROOM TAPPET
Allows higher lifts and higher rates of valve acceleration which are impossible to obtain on the stock 1" tappets. Makes a decided improvement in Volumetric Efficiency (Breathing Efficiency).

BACK SPOT FACING TOOL
Driven by ½" electric hand drill, 400 R.P.M. or slower.
Spot face should be only deep enough to allow mushroom basses to clear inside diameter of cam bearings by .020" and allow cam entry.

STROKED
Outer circle shows '49 Mercury with 4" stroke as compared with stock.

VALVE OPENING DIAGRAM
Here is graphically portrayed the far superior advantage of the mushroom cam over the conventional racing cam. The shaded area indicates the relative increase in volumetric efficiency (breathing efficiency).

Mushroom Cam

Conventional Full Race Cam

LIFT

CRANK ROTATION DEGREES

Mushroom Cam

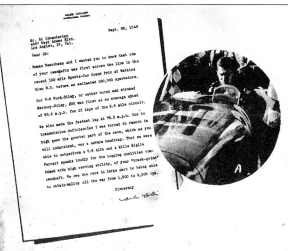

MILES COLLIER
INTERLOCHEN, FLORIDA

Sept. 26, 1949

Mr. Ed Iskenderian
4807 West Adams Blvd.
Los Angeles, 16, Cal.

Dear Ed:

Roman Beauchamp and I wanted you to know that one
of your camshafts was first across the line in the
recent 100 mile Sports-Car Grand Prix at Watkins
Glen N.Y. before an estimated 100,000 spectators.

Our V-8 Ford-Riley, or rather bored and stroked
Mercury-Riley, #89 was first at an average speed
of 68.5 m.p.h. for 15 laps of the 6.6 mile circuit.

We also made the fastest lap at 76.3 m.p.h. Due to
transmission deficiencies I was forced to remain in
high gear the greater part of the race, which as you
will understand, was a severe handicap. That we were
able to outperform a 2.6 Alfa and a Mille Miglia
Ferrari speaks loudly for the lugging qualities combined with high revving ability, of your "track-grind"
camshaft. We owe the race in large part to being able
to obtain wallop all the way from 1,500 to 5,500 rpm.

Sincerely,

Champions and Record Holders Using Iskenderian Cams

A. **Miles Collier—Winner of Watkins** Glen New York Grand Prix.

B. George Zimmer's "Skeemon Demon" racing cracker box boat which raised the official world's record by 15 miles per hour.

C. Mensing Brothers' V8-60 midget. Winner of Iowa State Championship and top purse winners of 1949.

D. Frank Litwin, owner, and Red Cummings, driver, winner of 1948 and 1949 New England modified stock car championship.

IN 1950, THIS BROCHURE WAS THE STATE OF THE ART LITERATURE IN THE RACING CAM INDUSTRY.

THE "LEON COOK" AD AGENCY PRODUCED IT, IN ONLY THREE DAYS, JUST IN TIME TO DISTRIBUTE AT THE FIRST EVER HOT ROD SHOW IN THE LOS ANGELES ARMORY.

BOB BARSKY HIRED THE YOUNG BOB PETERSEN AND BOB LINSLAY TO SCOUT THE TOWN FOR THE BEST HOT RODS TO DISPLAY.

THIS ASSOCIATION INSPIRED THEM TO START THE FIRST HOT ROD MAGAZINE.

WE ARE GRATEFUL TO C.A.STEVENS, STEVENS RACING ENTERPRISES, SOMIS, CALIFORNIA, FOR PRESERVING THIS ORIGINAL, WHICH WE HAVE REPRODUCED HERE.

NOTE: THIS DRAWING MADE BY JOHN "PRESLEY" ATHAN

the new cam, and the selection of other components, such as pistons, lifters, push rods, and compression ratios. Any Isky catalog packs a ton of information for just $5, although in earlier days, they were as little as a quarter.

For someone who never went to college, much less took any marketing or business classes in school, Isky proved to be particularly savvy and instinctive at this aspect of running his business. He also realized the substantial promotional value of having race-winning cars using his products and advertising that fact on their racer's fenders and doors. That also led to a particularly interesting form of advertising and product promotion that was seen as new and innovative at the time, but is now commonly accepted and largely ubiquitous today.

The Harrison and Lean Model A roadster helped inspire the notion of racing sponsorship T-shirts as we know them today. It's highly likely that Isky was the first to do this, beginning with this modest effort in 1951. Nobody knows where this car is today or if it still exists, but there must be tens of thousands of Isky T-shirts out there. This little car was truly the start of something big. (Photo Courtesy Ed Iskenderian)

Giving You the Shirt on Your Back

The first car sponsored by Iskenderian Racing Cams was a stock-bodied '32 Ford roadster run at the 1951 SCTA meet held on the Bonneville Salt Flats near Wendover, Utah, built and driven by Doug Harrison and Norm Lean. The car ran an Isky cam; it received parts and possibly modest financial support from Isky.

A night or two before they were to compete, the team owners mentioned to Ed that they wanted to "dress up the crew a little bit." So they went to a T-shirt shop

This fabulous photo was snapped some years after the "Isky T-shirt" was born at Bonneville in 1951, but you get the idea. This great scene comes from the 1958 NHRA Nationals (fourth annual) in Oklahoma City, Oklahoma. That's the Buck & Bohls '29 A roadster, with a six-carb Olds V-8, from Austin, Texas, versus Joe Yeamon's Chrysler Hemi-powered '27 T from Grand Junction, Colorado. Notice that the shirts on the backs of these young lads boast about Isky's part legendary, yet somewhat mythical "5-cycle" camshaft technology. (Photo Courtesy Pat Ganahl)

in Hollywood and had some T-shirts silk-screen printed to include the name of the car and the Isky Racing Cams name and logo. Nobody else was doing this at the time, although it's commonly seen today in and around the pits or the grandstands at any form of motorsports. Branded racing t-shirts are as common as beer sales at the concessions stands.

Isky thought the idea was absolute magic and wanted to have this sort of promotional tool available for his company, thinking that other racing teams that he sponsored and customers might be willing to wear these shirts, thus "flying the flag" for his brand and products. He designed new shirts that displayed his company name and logo much more prominently, and they became a much-desired "brand premium."

"We also tried hats with our name and logo on them," Isky recalls, "and still offer them, but they just didn't seem as popular as the shirts. Maybe it's because hats sometimes blow off, or a guy takes his hat off to work under his car and they just disappear. But everyone went crazy for these shirts."

Isky doesn't take absolute credit for being the first aftermarket high-performance parts company to advertise on T-shirts, but he may have been the first to do so on a large scale basis, or at minimum, *among* the very first. To this day, more than 60 years later, you can contact the company and, for a small fee, get a wonderful Isky Racing Cams "care package" containing printed materials, an Ed Iskenderian and his hot rod "hero" photo, logo stickers, and (you guessed it) an Isky-branded T-shirt.

This well-staged and immaculately detailed photo was assuredly shot for a Hot Rod *or* Car Craft *engine-building feature. The shiny, injected V-8 is a nailhead Buick, and the shirt is from 1964, hailing Isky's successful 505 Magnum cam, and also celebrating the 1964 NHRA Winternationals in Pomona, California. (Photo Courtesy Pat Ganahl)*

Chapter 4

GROWING THE BUSINESS AND THE INDUSTRY

Ed believed very much in his long-duration, high-overlap 5-cycle cam and put it straight to the test on the racetrack. This is drag racer Ted Cyr, photographed in May 1958 at Lions' Associated Drag Strip during the Chrondek Progressive races. This is a Cyr/Hopper dragster, a milestone car. "Isky Cams 5 Cycle Special" is painted on only this side. "U-Fab Manifolds" is painted on the other side of the car. (Photo Courtesy TEN: The Enthusiast Network Archive)

Iskenderian's fledgling company was already beginning to grow as 1949 became 1950. The new year ushered in a new postwar prosperity, the birth and expansion of the speed parts industry, and ever better-performing new cars rolling off the production lines in Detroit, boasting new engine designs that just begged for the performance makeover. Ed's business was born around the design and production of high-performance cams for the trusty Ford flathead V-8, but by this time it was clear that the flathead's days as a frontline production engine for a large and varied organization such as the Ford Motor Company were coming to a close.

Furthermore, even just keeping up with the demand for flathead cams quickly outstripped the capability of Ed's two-man, one-machine company. He needed more equipment to produce more product, and more room in which to do it. He moved locations several times in and around the industrial communities of greater South Los Angeles: Los Angeles, Culver City, Inglewood, and ultimately Gardena.

In 1946, not long after setting up shop in the back room at his friend John Athan's Mercury Tool and Die, Isky relocated the company to the West Adams area of Los Angeles, where the shop remained until 1950. In addition to continuing to serve the performance demand of those racers and rodders that still ran the Ford flathead, Isky was fortuitous in that Detroit's big carmakers were developing new and more advanced V-8 engines for use in new postwar models that were begging to go racing.

What's That Flying Overhead?

Oldsmobile and Cadillac each introduced new, relatively high-performance overhead valve V-8s for the 1949 model year. Even though their pushrod and rocker arm valvetrains are more complicated than the old-style flatheads, they generally breathe more efficiently. Even stock, the engines were very good; the Oldsmobile Rocket 88 model was seen as the original muscle car of its day, and the Cadillac OHV instantly became a popular race car powerplant and a favorite of engine swappers. More than a few "Fordillacs" (Ford bodies or hot rods running Cadillac engines) and "Studillacs" (the same principle except employing a Studebaker chassis/body) were built at the time.

Isky immediately went to work developing higher-performance camshaft profiles for both engines, and the market proved to be particularly ripe when it was discovered that, when used in high-performance or racing situations, the stock camshafts (particularly in Oldsmobile V-8s) wore out quickly under high-performance use and racing conditions.

Iskenderian was happy to grind up brand new cams, beginning with stock camshaft blanks (the raw iron stock used to create a new camshaft) and also offered to "regrind" the stock camshaft to a more aggressive profile. Unfortunately, these early reground cams weren't any longer lived than the stock production piece, because the alloy of the metal was a bit too soft for the rigors of high performance. So Isky developed an innovative way to fortify the metal on the cam's lobe surfaces for it to wear a higher-performance profile and offer improved longevity. He called the approach "hard-facing."

This involved grinding a narrow groove into the "nose" of the cam lobe. Then, using a gas welder and a specially alloyed welding rod, Ed's gang would build up a ridge of metal running right down the middle of each cam lobe, and then the cam would be ground back down to the proper new high-performance profile with the correct valve lift and duration specifications. This specially alloyed welding rod was of a much harder material than the camshaft underneath it and gave the

One look at the Chrysler Hemi's spark plug placement in the middle of its oversized valvecovers and you can tell that this Ardun-converted flathead was clearly a design inspiration. The Ardun did a lot for the old flatty, really waking up its breathing and thus its torque and horsepower outputs. Another aspect that made the Ardun so exotic in its day is that the hemispherical overhead valve heads are cast aluminum; not something many American engine cylinder heads could claim.

This example is particularly exotic because it wears a rare S.Co.T. (Supercharger Company of Turin) supercharger. This engine would look fabulous in any hot rod or period racing car. (Photo Courtesy Steve Magnante)

What's In a Name?

When Ed launched his business, he did so under the obvious, if somewhat formal, name of Ed Iskenderian Racing Cams. After a while, he dropped his first name from advertisements and such, the company more often referred to as Iskenderian Racing Cams. He'd been nicknamed "Isky" as a kid for obvious reasons, and in the 1960s, it simply became "Isky Racing Cams." The latter was catchy, easy to remember, and easy to spell, and it fit better on T-shirts, stickers, and the variety of all-important promotional tools that Ed increasingly used as his company grew.

This ad must have come along in 1955 or 1956 because it offers a high-performance valvetrain kit for the Ford 312 Y-block engine, which was first available in the 1956 Thunderbird; when first Thunderbird was introduced in 1955, it ran a 292 Y-block. The company was still called Ed Iskenderian Racing Cams at this point. (Photo Courtesy Ed Iskenderian)

cam a longer usable life than the original underlying "too soft" material.

For this method to work its best, Ed recommended the customer switch to "chilled iron" lifters, a material better suited to the new profile and material of the reground, "hard-faced" camshaft. Although this method likely didn't last as long as a new camshaft, when ground from scratch on properly hardened and alloyed metal, it allowed the customer to switch to a higher-performance camshaft profile, avoid the premature wear issue, and save money all at the same time, because to hard face and regrind the customer's own cam cost less than buying new from scratch.

It quickly became a popular product for the company and Ed expanded it to other engines, but he was concerned about protecting the somewhat proprietary nature of this process. So deliveries and payments took place in a rather "back alley" fashion. His biggest concern was that other camshaft companies would catch on to the idea and rush to purchase mass quantities of the special welding rod used for it. Therefore, he made deals with various metal supply houses to sell it only to him and, at the same time, purchased large inventories of this material so he always had plenty on hand.

Ultimately, cam regrinding and hard-facing became a meaningful aspect of the company's business. In some cases it was the sole subject of a few of its advertisements.

More New Engine Designs

The Detroit production engine scene continued to evolve throughout the 1950s. Besides the new Olds and Cadillac engines, Ford developed and launched its "Y-block" overhead valve engine for 1954, making 1953 the final year of production for the venerable flathead V-8. Chrysler waited a bit before rolling out all new V-8s, and Chevrolet, says Isky, "changed the world with the launch of the original small-block Chevy in 1955."

Ed shares interesting anecdotes about the design and development of the first generation, early Chrysler Hemi V-8, and a special version of the new Chevrolet V-8. Keep in mind that it wasn't at all unusual for racers and rodders to replace the cylinder heads on their Model T and Model A engines with entire new pieces produced by companies such as Rajo, Frontenac, and Cragar. As the flathead V-8 became ever more popular among racers and rodders alike, a number of companies came up with high-performance replacement heads for them as well, including Edelbrock, Meyer, Offenhauser, Edmunds, and a host of others. So, upmarket heads were common.

One particularly interesting option for the flathead was an overhead valve conversion package called Ardun. These were designed by and named for the brilliant engineer and racing driver Zora Arkus-Duntov, a name you may recognize as the soon-to-be chief engineer and product manager for the Chevrolet Corvette.

These innovative heads relocated all of the valves out of the flathead block up into the heads, for a complete overhead valve conversion. The heads also employed a "hemispherical" combustion chamber design, believed to be much more efficient than a standard overhead valve combustion chamber because of its unique placement of the spark plug within the head and between the valves, rather than somewhat off to the side of the chamber as in most conventional heads.

Regardless, these aftermarket Ardun heads employed this "hemi" head design, which no American carmaker was using them on a production V-8 at the time. So, according to Isky, when Chrysler commissioned a group of engineers to begin designing an overhead valve V-8 to replace its long-running flathead straight-8 engine, a couple of the young, talented, performance-minded engineers began to study engine block and head designs. They stumbled upon the Ardun and felt that this innovative head and combustion

Chrysler's big Hemi was a huge watershed item for street performance, drag racing, and top speed racing at Bonneville. The hemispherical heads, which put the spark plugs in the middle of the combustion chamber, resulted in these large and positively exotic-looking valvecovers. Appropriately, Chrysler called them FirePower.

chamber design would perhaps be ideal for the new Chrysler V-8.

Again, Ed recalls that more than a few Ardun heads ended up on the desks and drawing tables of Chrysler's engine developers and is quite sure this activity led to the birth of Chrysler's first generation "Fire Power" Hemi-head V-8 in 1950 for the 1951 model year. It is also true that hemispherical combustion chambers were used in some military aircraft and tank engine designs during the World War II era.

It was employed to great effect in a variety of early Chrysler and DeSoto models and became an all-conquering racing engine (with a substantial number of them running Iskenderian cams). Later generations of the Hemi powered the most successful and now sought after Chrysler, Dodge, and Plymouth muscle cars of the 1960s and 1970s.

The previously mentioned Belgian-born American engineer Zora Arkus-Duntov ultimately became known as "the father of the Corvette," a worthy if somewhat misleading nickname because he didn't come up with the idea for the Corvette, and never claimed sole rights to its development. But it's fair to say that not long after joining General Motors in 1953, Arkus-Duntov taught the Corvette how to go fast and win races, earning for decades the title of "America's one true sports car" and cementing him as "The Vettefather."

Isky recalls another interesting story about Arkus-Duntov: the development of a special high-performance version of the small-block Chevy V-8 and its very unique camshaft design. When Zora joined GM, the Corvette had one powertrain to its name, the triple-carbureted Blue Flame inline-6 backed by a 2-speed Powerglide automatic transmission.

Being a hot rodder and racer with some European sensibilities, Arkus-Duntov felt that this powertrain was all wrong for a proper sports car. He, of course, knew of Chevrolet's upcoming-for-1955 265-ci V-8 and made sure he had his collective arms around it for installation into the Corvette

It took little more than a glance at an Ardun-headed flathead to see the original Chrysler Hemi's similarity to it. The valvetrain architecture between them is a bit different, and the Ardun heads are cast aluminum, while the Chrysler Hemi is all cast iron. No history book that I've read cites the Ardun as a clear progenitor of the Mopar engine, but the similarities are startling. Isky spent a lot of time talking with factory engineers and racers back then, and is quite sure of his version of the story.

as an option for 1955, along with a manual transmission (although it was still just a 3-speed at this point; no 4-speeds until mid-1957). This was just the start of the Corvette's ever-increasing performance levels. The engine was due to expand to 283 ci for 1957, and he wanted special high-performance versions of it for the car he was in charge of.

Isky recalls that Arkus-Duntov was aware of the legendary engine wizard Ed Winfield, and remembers equally that the GM engineer consulted with Winfield on a souped-up 283 small-block. This special 283 was conceived with road racing in mind; somewhat European in that it would wear dual 4-barrel carburetors and employ adjustable mechanical "solid" lifters to allow for sustained high-RPM running and good mid-range and top-end power.

Of course, a specially configured camshaft was needed for the job. Arkus-Duntov and Winfield worked together to design a special profile that took into account the 283's breathing habits, the dual carburetors, and the relatively high compression. This particular engine option, initially rated at 245 hp, was nicknamed the Duntov 283, and its special camshaft became colloquially named "the Duntov Cam." This camshaft is still popular and available today from Chevrolet and a variety of other companies that still sell that exact profile.

Not for a minute does Isky minimize Arkus-Duntov's genius or ability to develop this engine, but notes this camshaft insider's bit of trivia about Ed Winfield's involvement in this famous component and engine combination.

Finally, a Shop to Call Home

As Iskenderian's business grew, he added employees and equipment. This meant his needs for shop space increased

Isky's compact shop was at 6338 Slauson Avenue in Culver City, California. It's difficult to tell exactly what year this photo was taken, but judging by the cars parked in front or driving by, it's likely to have been snapped sometime in the early 1950s. (Photo Courtesy Ed Iskenderian)

Isky's Slauson Avenue shop building still exists, although the area around it has changed dramatically, with much newer retail construction. The building is only used for storage these days. You may wonder why it still carries Isky's signage and lettering? Simple enough: the building is owned by Isky's longtime pal John Athan, who rents it out to a neighboring business owner; he never saw the need to whitewash Iskenderian's name off the front visage. (Photo Courtesy Ed Iskenderian)

considerably. His first few locations were rented space, and several expansions meant relocation.

After that back room at John Athan's Mercury Tool and Die, Ed took space in a few other small shops before moving to the West Adams area of Los Angeles. But by 1950, he needed to move again, and he decided it was time to buy his own property and build his own shop.

He found the spot on Slauson Avenue in Culver City, just off of Jefferson Blvd. He bought a small commercial lot for $2,000 (if you can imagine that) and built a new building from scratch for about $8,000; he occupied this building from 1951 to 1958. That little box of a shop space is significant for a variety of reasons, but the most significant is that it put Isky's business across the street from Vic Edelbrock's garage and race shop.

At the time, Edelbrock had already begun making a name for himself by producing high-performance intake manifolds and heads, mostly for the Ford flathead V-8 and the slightly miniaturized version of it, the V-8 60. The V-8 60 was architecturally similar to the standard Ford flathead but was about two-thirds the size and had become a popular engine choice for midget racing and transplanting into small imported sports cars normally powered by 4-cylinder engines.

The V-8 60 was an extremely popular engine for Midget racing cars, and Edelbrock Sr. ran one in his Midget racer. Edelbrock did not produce camshafts at the time, and Isky did not produce intake manifolds, so the two were naturally complementary businesses. The pair knew each other from dry lakes racing circles and were friends.

"We were good friends, Vic and I. We knew each other as kids and raced our cars against each other at the dry lakes. His car was fast and ran really well, at least 120 on most days if I remember. My Model T was a little lighter than his '32 roadster, so after getting up to speed I could run about as fast as he could, but he was still quicker on the top end." Isky says. He idolizes Edelbrock and credits him with being highly innovative and a trustworthy friend with whom to do business.

"I knew Vic before he even made his own intake manifolds, when he was still helping with development work for Thickstun, another early manifold maker."

Also helpful to Isky and his business needs is that Edelbrock had an engine dynamometer in his shop. This device accurately measures an engine's horsepower and torque outputs, allowing component makers such as Isky and Edelbrock to test and prove that a new (or a competitor's) camshaft or intake manifold did, or did not, produce the power increase that was anticipated. Edelbrock allowed Isky to use his dyno, a considerable advantage in the development of new cam profiles. Edelbrock became an Iskenderian distributor and often listed Isky's cams in his catalogs and advertising.

The Power of Advertising

Ed has always been a huge believer in the power of advertising, promotion, and good public relations. He advertised as much as he could afford in the magazines and racing newspapers. In addition, he felt that a magazine ad, when possible, should be a combination of product announcement and/or promotion, a certain whimsy or sense of humor (this aspect ably dealt with by his creative consultant Pete Millar, the guy responsible for the cartoonish illustrations seen in many Isky ads), and information to benefit the reader.

The latter was accomplished in a variety of ways; sometimes, Ed invested up to a quarter of a full-page ad to pass along technical advice to the reader, who was also, of course, his potential customer. Called "Top Tuner's Tips," he often wrote these tech passages himself.

Sometimes the length and breadth of these technical passages far outstripped the size of a quarter of a magazine page, so the company would publish them as a

Edelbrock Power and Speed Equipment was pretty well established by the time Isky went into business. It was likely a big boon to the small camshaft maker that his products were advertised nationwide by a company as prestigious and well respected as Edelbrock. (Photo Courtesy Edelbrock LLC)

separate, multipage technical paper, and then advertise that paper in his ad spread. The information was ostensibly free, as you could get the company's technical paper on a variety of topics, such as "Valve Timing for Maximum Output," for just $1 postage paid.

Ed and his creative advertising and marketing team developed a variety of fun and unusual names for the company's products. The original flathead Ford V-8 cam was called the 404, and some versions the 404-JR. Then came the wonderful Polydyne cam, the 5-cycle cam (an interesting claim at the time, considering most conventional engines then and now are based around a four-cycle combustion process), plus the 505 Magnum cam, the

Ed was investing heavily by running full-page ads in many hot rod and racing magazines; this ad is from the pages of Hot Rod in 1966. Note the car of the month and Isky's "Top Tuner's Tips." (Photo Courtesy Ed Iskenderian)

If Ed's "Top Tuner's Tips" was too comprehensive to publish in a quarter of an ad page, he'd publish it as a stand-alone technical paper, which, of course, the reader or potential customer could get free, except for the cost of postage. (Photo Courtesy Ed Iskenderian)

This elegant "Touring of Milano, Superleggera" badge sits atop the trunk of a Lamborghini GT350, which I can assure you does not run Isky cams. Ed's misspelled Super Le Gerra cam designation came about because he felt the name sounded cool and knew it had something to do with Italian cars.

Parabolic, and the Revmaster, and among my favorites, the Super Le Gerra. This is an odd and slightly misspelled adaptation of a body and chassis construction method pioneered by coachbuilder Touring of Milan, Italy, and had nothing to do with camshaft design or going faster other than by virtue of lighter vehicle weight.

The principle behind the original Touring Superlegerra (which, loosely translated from Italian, means "super light") concept was that of lightweight aluminum body panels affixed to a skeleton frame of small diameter steel tubing welded together to create an exoskeleton of the car's shape, to be clothed and finished with the hand-shaped body panels. Leave it to Isky to adopt and modify the name of an Italian body construction method to hot rod and racing camshafts.

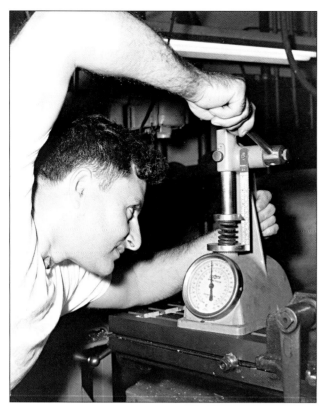

Ed never intended to go into the valvespring business. Initially, he provided heavier-duty springs at cost and as a customer service to cam buyers. After a while, as engines became ever more powerful and revved higher and higher, valvesprings were often a weak link in the valvetrain. Therefore, Ed began offering a comprehensive line of single, double, and, in some cases, triple valvesprings to take the punishment served up by super-high-winding V-8s at the dragstrip or Bonneville.

Here Ed measures valvespring tension on a manually operated dial machine, which is done on computerized machinery today. Isky was always happy to fly old school. (Photo Courtesy TEN: The Enthusiast Network Archive)

First the Cam, Now the Kit

"It wasn't very long into the high-performance cam-grinding business that we learned of the need for high-performance valvesprings, because the hot cams allowed the engine to rev faster and higher so it opened the door to ways to expand our business and give the customer something that worked better." As with most things in his business, he learned based on his experience with flatheads. "Our fast-action flathead cams really punished the stock valvesprings, so we cast around for springs that were firmer and that lasted longer."

As with many things, he found the answer in a related Ford product. "We discovered that the Lincoln Zephyr flathead V-12 engine had tougher springs that fit right into the Ford V-8, and seemed to run better and last longer, so we started using those. In the case of the Oldsmobile Rocket-88 cam that we hard-faced and reground into a hotter cam, we found that

a 1938–1940 Cadillac flathead V-8 spring was the perfect answer. It dropped right into the Olds head with no modifications and must have had a little higher rating, because it kept the valves from floating. So we bought them from Cadillac and had them in stock for the Olds cam customer."

At this point, about 1950 to 1951, Iskenderian bought the springs directly from Cadillac, and their cost was about 75 cents per spring, and he just passed them on to the customer at cost. Thus, the "cam and kit" was born. Ed doesn't take credit for inventing the notion of selling associated valvetrain gear along with his cams as the pure invention of buying a "cam and kit" of associated parts, but he's pretty sure his company was among the earliest players at doing this.

"And after a while, we figured out we could buy the Cadillac springs directly from the company that produced them for GM. We investigated the idea of buying direct from them, and they checked to make sure they had no exclusive arrangement in their

ISKY RACING CAMS

NEW!

the *HPx*™ SERIES *(Hydraulic Performance Xtreme)*
Featuring "Best on the Planet" Super-Precision Johnson/SEC® Quality!

ABSOLUTE 100% MADE IN THE U.S.A. GUARANTEE

HPx™ NEEDLE BEARING

The World's Finest Hydraulic Roller Lifters!

HPx™ EZ-ROLL™ NEEDLE FREE!

SILVER	PERFORMANCE LEVEL	GOLD
	Features:	
✓	PDQ Hi-Flow Valving™	✓
✓	Ultra Super Precision Mfg.	✓
✓	Hear No "Tick"™/Johnson® Quality	✓
✓	Anti-Flex Defense™	✓
	Anti-Lock *EZ-Roll*™ Bearings	✓
	The Big Foot Effect™	✓
	Triple Rolling Immunity™	✓
	Patented Vortex-Wave™	✓

Standard *HPx*™ Package

EZ-Roll™ Upgrade

Isky's friend, the hardworking and wheelchair-bound Chet Herbert, launched the modern-day adoption of "roller" camshafts, lifters, and pushrods. Ed originally thought that Herbert adopted this style of needle-bearing roller assemblies from Harley-Davidson racing motorcycles of the day but was later reminded that this was something Herbert did for race-modified GMC 6-cylinder truck engines. (Photo Courtesy Ed Iskenderian)

Isky cranking on an Edelbrock-equipped flathead; presumably, it was also equipped with an Isky cam. Note the large, chrome remote oil filter mounted on top of the engine and the cool dual carbs. This flatty is rigged up on the dynamometer that Ed bought from Vic Edelbrock Sr. (Photo Courtesy Edelbrock LLC)

The Cam Wars

Ed doesn't remember when the cam wars really started, but he recalls it being in full swing by the mid-1950s. The performance cam–grinding business had some roots in pre–World War II hot rodding, but really took off with the start of the post-war peace in 1945, and new car production got back to business for 1946. So many of the dry lakes racer types, who fooled around with developing their own cam designs, got into the cam business with a supply of military surplus machining equipment, not to mention the thousands of GIs returning home with mechanical and machining skills who were ready and looking for work.

But the cam business really started honking in the 1950s, and it became very competitive. Isky recalls, "Most of us were friends, so a lot of it was sort of 'friendly competition.' Yet for some of the players, it was very unfriendly." And Isky was in the thick and middle of it. It was primarily an ongoing joust between Isky and Howard Johansen's Howards Cams. Occasionally, another manufacturer would join in. The battlefields were primarily SCTA Bonneville salt flat racing and NHRA drag racing.

This is where the races and wars were won and lost, but the competition played out largely in the advertising pages of *Hot Rod* and countless other drag racing and land speed record racing magazines and newspapers that sprang up to fill the demand for information on the growth of these two sports, and the technology that drove the cars faster and faster.

Isky recalls, "Every month, one cam company or another claimed to be the best or the world's fastest [Isky often among them] in some category or another, and we played along too. Which makes sense; otherwise, why would any of us provide products to racing teams and put our names and stickers on their cars if we didn't boast about the wins a little bit?"

He also recalls that once, someone came up with an idea that the wins and bragging rights should be spread around among them, with one company being able to make the "world's best" claims one month, and then the next month another team "gets to win" and hold the claims and title for a month, and so forth. Upon some thought, Isky realized this was too much like fixing boxing matches or horse racing and not good for the sport or business. He declined to participate and isn't sure this rigging plan ever got off the ground in any measure. It's just as well.

The cam wars continued well into the 1960s as more and more companies joined the business, and Isky enjoyed much of the fight. *Hot Rod* magazine fills in some of the blanks about the wars: "Isky is well remembered for his involvement in the 'cam wars' of the 1950s, the back-and-forth advertising campaign he waged with Howard Johansen of Howard Cams. Isky created and advertised a '5-cycle' cam, labeling the overlap period in the cam timing as the fifth cycle. Of course, Johansen made fun of it in his ads, (one in particular showing four bicycles being ridden together in a line, going in one direction, with each cycle numbered one through four.

"Then there was a number-5 bicycle being ridden by a clown (poking at Isky's notion of the 5-cycle cam), and Isky would give it right back to him in his ads. It was a legendary but mostly good-natured ribbing between the two Los Angeles-based cam grinders that probably couldn't happen in today's litigious, politically correct society."

Isky and his famous roadster in front of his Inglewood, California, shop. Note that the car looks particularly fresh here, with gleaming, polished valvecovers, intake stacks, and exhaust, with shiny black paint on the charming Model T "turtle deck" bodywork. (Photo Courtesy Ed Iskenderian)

contract with Cadillac to prohibit them from selling direct to us, so we started buying them (I don't recall the company's name) at 35 cents a spring, and still sold them to our customer at 75 cents each, which is what he'd pay at any Cadillac dealer or speed shop. So the cost to customer was the same, but we began making a little more money on the deal, and the customer received a more complete package."

The notion of the "cam and kit" has ebbed and flowed a bit over time, but now most cams are purchased with associated valvesprings, rockers, lifters, pushrods, and sometimes more componentry that is all matched to work together.

It wasn't long before Chet Herbert, one of Isky's friends in the business, began producing "roller" camshafts, which more accurately means roller lifters, and that gave birth to the need for adjustable pushrods. The idea behind the use of roller bearings was to reduce mechanical friction and drag, and the parasitic power losses that come with them. Isky recalls, "Chet only had one cam-grinding

machine, and thus was limited to about one or two roller cams and kits per day. After a while, I had the resources to produce six to eight roller cams and kits per day. I asked him if it was okay if I jumped onto this bandwagon for a bit, and he said fine since he couldn't keep up with demand, and since I could, he was happy to see us get the business."

As he began to develop products for more and more types of engines, he needed more testing time on a reliable engine dynamometer. His friend Vic Edelbrock had been most generous in allowing Ed to run over with a cam or an engine and mount it all up to Vic's dyno, but it was clear that Ed needed his own machine. Vic believed he could make good use of a newer and higher-capacity machine, so he bought new equipment and sold his existing dyno to Isky. This expanded Ed's horizons considerably; he could test new product developments immediately at his own shop at any time of the day or night to keep the development ball rolling. Plus, he was deeply embroiled in the "cam wars."

Of all the interesting people who have worked for Ed over the decades, it's doubtful any has contributed more to his success, or accomplished more, than Robert "Bones" Balough. Bones worked for Isky for about six years, running the dyno testing and helping to develop a lot of winning cam profiles.

Here Ed and Bones mug with one of the racing jackets Isky Racing Cams gave out to all of its 27 class winners at the 1962 Indy Nationals. (Photo Courtesy Ed Iskenderian)

The Infamous 5-Cycle Cam

Ah, the 5-cycle cam. Isky recalls, "This goes back a ways. Scotty Fenn built a dragster chassis and sold it to Cook and Bedwell in San Diego. They came to me and got a free cam for their Chrysler 331 and put a Crower manifold with eight carburetors on it. Emery Cook used to talk with a lot of authority, but he didn't know a lot about engines, I could tell.

"One day he said to me, 'Isky, why don't you make a five-cycle cam like the Italians do?' And I thought, gee, that'd be a heck of a good publicity stunt, but how could I justify a fifth combustion cycle? Oh, it'd have to be the overlap period. That would have to be doing some good.

"I had studied some of the cams and combustion cycles on Alfa Romeos and some of the other Italian sports and racing cars, and noticed that they have a lot of 'overlap,' which is the angle in crankshaft degrees when both the intake and exhaust valves are open. This occurs at the end of the exhaust stroke and the beginning of the intake stroke. Increasing lift duration and/or decreasing lobe separation increases overlap.

"So I started playing that up with customers and in my advertising. All of a sudden, Cook and Bedwell went 11 mph over the speed record, which was 155 roughly. At the time you couldn't go much faster than that."

The period from 1958 to 1959 was a critically important and fast-moving time for Isky and his company. As the 1950s progressed, Iskenderian Racing Cams grew from a one man, one machine back-room operation to a full-fledged business that continued to outgrow its locations. So in 1958, Ed built a new from-scratch facility at 607 N. Inglewood Avenue in Inglewood, California.

It was around 20,000 square feet of offices, showroom, production factory, testing area, warehouse, and shipping and receiving. Vic Edelbrock Jr. called it a "first-class operation" at the time. Ed was in full command of his business, but also had a wife and kids so he didn't do much racing anymore; his business, his

This photo illustrates the "egg cam" inspiration that ultimately became the successful 505 Magnum profile. It worked well in a variety of engines but proved to be particularly hot in small-block Chevys. (Photo Courtesy Mel Stone)

family, and a little fishing now and again consumed most of his daylight. He had a building full of employees now, produced camshafts and a wide variety of high-performance valvetrain products, and had his own dynamometer on which to test and evaluate his products.

One day, a tall, handsome young man heard, from outside the building, an engine screaming away on the dyno and knocked on the door to ask what was making all the noise and why.

That man turned out to be Robert "Bones" Balough, who worked night shift at the nearby Douglas Aircraft factory. Bones was born in Pennsylvania, then settled in Long Beach, California, after World War II. He asked Isky if "the guy who ran that engine machine was paid to do it." When Isky replied that he was, in fact, paid for the job, Bones said, "That looks like so much fun I'd probably do it for free."

Ed is at his desk in Inglewood. "Nice and messy, just how I like it," he says. What is amazing is that he can almost always find something when he needs it. (Photo Courtesy TEN: The Enthusiast Network Archive)

A young Vic Edelbrock Jr. working on a dual-carb Mercury Y-block V-8. It's possible that this engine was equipped with the factory-offered "power kit" that was developed by Edelbrock and Isky. (Photo Courtesy TEN: The Enthusiast Network Archive)

Isky liked his attitude and invited him to come back the next day for an interview and to talk about it. By chance, the employee Isky had running the dyno was leaving in about a month's time, so he hired Balough on the spot. It turned out to be a magical match-up. Bones began learning how to accurately perform and document the dyno runs, but wondered why the machine was only rated at 4,500 rpm maximum, because, of course, racing engines often turned much higher RPM than that, and he needed to be able to increase and verify power well beyond 4,500. So Bones began to push the machine a bit.

One day, after the engine and the machine were well warmed up, he made a run up to 5,000. He kept pushing the machine and was soon making safe dyno pulls up to 7,000 with race-built small-block Chevy V-8s. He doesn't deny that he hit 7,500 rpm on more than a few occasions.

Isky and Bones both knew the value of this sort of testing, so Isky decided to expand the company's testing and evaluation capacity. He decided to step up to two dynos, with the hope of finding them used or surplus with capacity for well over his current machine's 4,500 revs rating. He did just that when he found a liquidation auction catalog in the mail one day for the sale of assets of the Scott Motors trucking company in Oakland, California. He and Balough went to Oakland and bought two virtually new engine dynos for the not-too-princely sum of $700 each, and took them back to Southern California to install.

He sold his old machine, the one formerly belonging to Vic Edelbrock, to a guy in New Jersey, whose name, shop name, or racing team he doesn't recall. He could now evaluate engines, cams, and valvetrain solutions side by side at any time of the day or night if he wished.

While all this was happening, Bones campaigned as a successful professional drag racer, having begun in 1955, and his career encompassed a varied portfolio of Gasser class and altered-wheelbase machines (obviously with many of them running Isky Cams), several business partners, and countless wins. It added up to great enough accomplishments to earn him an easy and well-deserved induction into the NHRA Hall of Fame.

Bones worked at Isky Racing Cams from late 1959 until 1966. He and Ed Iskenderian remain not only legends of speed but very good friends today.

As you've likely figured out by now, every cam-grinding wizard was constantly in search of the perfect cam lobe "profile" that would unlock the magic power within any given engine. Of course, induction, carburetion, ignition, timing, compression, and exhaust efficiency have great impacts on the power an engine can make, but given that the camshaft(s) is really the heartbeat and timing of an engine, the right cam can really let an engine loose, or bring it to its collective knees.

Cam experts find their inspiration in a variety of places, such as the cam profiles of other engines (particularly those in high-output race cars) or sometimes it's an idea in their heads that can be developed with much mathematical analysis. And at least in one case, for Ed Iskenderian and his chief dyno dude, Robert Bones Balough, their inspiration came from one of nature's humble and plentiful servants: the chicken.

Look at most cam lobes and you'll see that they are generally egg-shaped. Granted, the nose can be a bit pointier, or less, and the width of the "bump" on a chicken egg might be larger or smaller. But one day Isky and Bones were staring at eggs and wondered if there might be some secret buried in its shape. "Keep in mind," Isky reminds us, "Ed Winfield and several others already had 'soft action' cams that would rev high and produce top-end power. This was fine, but we soon learned that many engines wanted higher lift and even more duration time with the valves open.

"We examined the shape of an egg and it seemed to us that its shape might help meet those goals. So we ground up a test cam and ran it." It turned out that this nature-inspired cam lobe shape, with a bit of experimentation and massaging, worked well on high-winding small-block and later big-block Chevrolet V-8s. It went on to figure in several successful Isky cam designs; again proving that innovation is where you find it. Ed recalls that their first discovery and experimentation with egg-shaped cam lobes took place in 1961 to 1962.

Isky's friendship with Vic Edelbrock Sr. yielded much fruit over the years. One particular time was when Vic invited Isky to participate in a factory racing kit program being developed by Mercury for its versions of the Y-block V-8; even though it was architecturally a virtual twin to the Ford spec engine, the Mercury was often offered in larger displacements, and with different factory horsepower ratings, so Mercury wanted a performance kit of its own, not a clone of the Ford kit.

"That was a great deal that Vic brought me in on," Isky says today. "Vic was primarily in charge of subletting out the component work that his shop didn't do. He, of course, provided the intake manifold and some other parts, and we were brought in to develop the cams, springs, and some other bits. The big upside, besides it being a factory OEM-type deal, which for us was very prestigious, was that in order to qualify it or homologate it for production-type racing, the kit had to be manufactured in a quantity of at least 500 units.

"So that made a very nice parts order for us. Naturally, it took some hustle and overtime for us to meet the need, but it was a great job. We did our part, the cars ran great with this kit installed, and I'm pretty sure Mercury sold or gave out all 500 kits."

Chapter 5

ISKY CARS AND DRIVERS

This dramatic photo from Bonneville 1951 shows you what a stark and desolate place the salt flats really are. The nearest town is sleepy Wendover, but most hardcore types camp on the salt (although you won't see any Prevost motor homes there in the early 1950s). The famous Harrison and Lean Model A with '32 front bodywork is parked ahead of another equally red '32, and notice the rest of the cars: another pair of roadsters sitting behind the Deuces, plus a belly tanker (No. 111) to the far right of the shot, and a variety of civilian and support vehicles scattered about.

Bonneville stalwarts have said it's like "racing on the moon" because it's such a flat and featureless place. But, on good years, the surface is fast, and the lack of obstacles makes it as reasonably safe as it can be; lots of important history on this old ocean bed. (Photo Courtesy Bob Roddick Collection)

At 94 years old, and with more than 50 years of sponsoring cars under his belt, you would think Isky may not remember so many of the cars and drivers that wore his T-shirt, painted his name on the sides of their cars, or ran his camshafts. It's true he doesn't remember them all, but he recalls most with vivid clarity. From a business standpoint, it all comes back to the Harrison and Lean '32 roadster that he sponsored at that 1951 Bonneville meet, although by no means does Ed draw any significant line between the importance of Bonneville Land Speed Record (LSR) racing and drag racing when it comes to the value of advertising, promotion, and sponsorship; he's supported both genres equally over the years, although it's likely that professional drag racing has offered somewhat more commercial value.

In the case of the Harrison and Lean "T-shirt" '32, not only did he sponsor the car, but it is where the notion of the promotional T-shirt was born. He recalls that the driver and crew were a professional bunch that had it together and that the car ran well, although he doesn't recall it setting any record runs. No matter. It's a classic Deuce highboy, it was fast, and it had his name on the side.

Pat and Tony Berardini

Pat and Tony Berardini were a pair of handsome, clean-cut young brothers who ran a multifaceted automotive shop in South Central Los Angeles in the early 1950s. They handled general mechanical service, paint and body, and bought and sold used cars. The shop was a clean, honest place, and of course, the brothers were into racing. Isky Racing Cams could not have come up with better poster children for its company or products than Pat and Tony.

Among their fleet was this beautifully turned-out '32 roadster, and later a stripped-down '29 A/V8. Both brothers and cars used to compete regularly at Bonneville and in drag racing. Both cars were immaculate, although never intended to be show cars. They just looked that way because they were so well built and finished.

The '32 appears to have been flathead V-8 powered for much of its life, and the '29, over a period of years and owners, ran a variety of Ford and non-Ford engines; *Hot Rod* magazine estimates that over time, the pair won as much as 80 percent of their races. The '32 ran a hot-bored and stroked flathead but initially didn't run as fast as the brothers felt it should, so they switched to an Isky 404-JR. cam and the car just lit up.

The Berardinis retired from racing in 1955 and ultimately sold the '32 to a new owner, who kept and ran it in its original condition for some years prior to the installation of a 354-inch Chrysler Hemi. The car was later purchased by noted Kansas enthusiast and collector Roger Morrison, who in 2004 to 2005 commissioned a complete to-the-frame restoration, bringing the car back to nearly exact

Pat and Tony Berardini with their famous 404 '32 and only a few of its trophies. The brothers were winners more often than not, and this car earned several class championships. Note the beautifully fabbed, contoured roll bar just behind the driver's seat, which was something few cars had prior to the mid-1950s. (Photo Courtesy Roger Morrison Collection)

As classic a '32 roadster profile as you could imagine, although not a pure highboy style because it runs fenders. No matter, the rolling stock is perfect, as is the rake, stance, and ride height. This is one of the last photos taken of the car before it was sold to its second owner. You can see the round Iskenderian Racing Cams sticker on the black part of the cowl just below Pat's name. (Photo Courtesy Roger Morrison Collection)

What a great-looking pit crew! The car's new owner took this shot after the sale; his wife is posing at the front of the car. This fellow had different ideas about what the car should be; he later painted it metallic red and replaced the flathead with a Chrysler Hemi. (Photo Courtesy Roger Morrison Collection)

Ed and Pat Berardini grip and grin at an "open house" for the car after its acquisition by Roger Morrison and subsequent restoration. Pat was very emotional after the car was revealed post-restoration, pronouncing the job as "perfect" through joyful tears. And you can't miss the Isky Racing Cams sticker on the blocked-off grille plate. (Photo Courtesy Roger Morrison Collection)

Ed dives in for a close look at the hot flathead as the car is revealed at the Wally Parks NHRA museum in Pomona, California. Pat Berardini stands to Ed's right. Note the vintage four-carb intake. The workmanship everywhere is immaculate. (Photo Courtesy Roger Morrison Collection)

Ed couldn't resist the chance to hop into the Berardini 404 '32 and fire it up; the occasion was also caught on video and the car fired instantly and sounded hot. Obviously, Mr. 404 was really enjoying the noise. (Photo Courtesy Roger Morrison Collection)

specification; it was unveiled to a small group of friends including Pat Berardini, who was reduced to tears when the cover was pulled away, pronouncing the restoration "perfect" and commenting that "the car really got fast when we switched to that Isky 404 cam," which is the reason it wears race number 404.

It also made it to the National Roadster Show and other appearances beginning in 2005, and Isky was on hand for one of the receptions. Isky and Pat walked around the car for some time, then Isky hopped in and fired up the stout flathead. Apart from its abject beauty and authentic period-correct restoration, it's important to mention that the car won the S/R class drag racing championship from 1950 to 1955. The 404 remains a stunning combination of 1950s-style speed, beauty, guts, and success.

The Burbank Challenger

As LSR racing grew, the racers and car builders began to understand the impact of aerodynamics upon the car's body, handling, and speed. And of course many of them began learning the fundamentals of aerodynamics, "cheating the wind," and "slipstreaming," during their military service less than a decade before. All manner of aerodynamic experimentation began showing up at Bonneville and at the drag races in an effort to minimize the negative impact of the air and wind on their cars' performances.

At first this notion manifested itself in terms of hand-built "bullet-shaped" noses up front, hoping to reduce the car's frontal area (although they likely didn't know it was called that at the time), then came cars built with wind-cheating bodywork that

The Dean Batchelor–designed, Isky-cammed Spirit of Burbank *streamliner looks ready for its attack of the 1952 Bonneville salt. The car appears to be in the staging lanes, pre-run; the body is pristine and immaculate, with nary a hint of salt on the aerodynamic fiberglass panels. (Photo Courtesy Ed Iskenderian)*

The Davis-Hill team accepts the trophy for its exceptional runs on the salt that day in 1952. The team was not only competing with other Bonneville records, but also shooting to best records set in Europe by the vaunted Mercedes-Benz and Auto Union Teams. Impressive for a $3,000 car built in a home garage by a bunch of hot rodders. (Photo Courtesy Ed Iskenderian)

began life as a pointy-at-both-ends aircraft fuel tanks. These tanks were mounted to the bellies or under the wings of various military aircraft to increase their travel distance between refueling, often a critical issue in a long-range bombing mission. The fuel tanks were nicknamed "belly tanks," and they were often available postwar as military surplus items usually sold for pennies on the dollar.

The hot rodders and racers famously built cars inside, underneath, and around these aluminum tanks, hoping to find more speed by slipstreaming more easily through the air; so they were called belly tankers. It was discovered at the time that a car with a slipstreaming body and a long wheelbase could be more stable at high speeds, so the racers began building long chassis to be cloaked with streamlined body panels; these cars are most often referred to as "streamliners."

One such streamliner really rocked the salt in 1952, and it did so running an Isky cam. It's most commonly known as *Davis-Hill Special* (after owners/builders/drivers George Hill and Bill Davis), and has appeared in photographs over time wearing a variety of race numbers and sponsorship names on its fiberglass flanks. It was designed by noted hot rodder, car designer, racer, author, and journalist Dean Batchelor, and ran a single Ford flathead

Hill stands up for the team to take home the hardware. Isky was there and shot these photos on a small Brownie-style camera, back in the days of black-and-white film! (Photo Courtesy Ed Iskenderian)

V-8 engine equipped with CT Automotive overhead valve conversion heads.

Isky recalls that the builders asked him to supply a special cam aimed at helping the OHV flathead put out top power at maximum RPM. Unlike a street-driven hot rod and part-time racer, the streamliner pilot had no need or concern for low-RPM power, torque, or smoothness for fuel economy; it was all about maximum revs and top-end power, period.

The Davis-Hill streamer received more than its share of post-Bonneville ink, in the form of feature stories and cover photos for Hot Rod. . . (Photo Courtesy TEN: The Enthusiast Network Archive)

HOP UP

DECEMBER, 1952 ᵏ **20 CENTS**

LET'S TAKE A RIDE IN A FULL
RACE STREET ROADSTER!
See Hop Up Road Test, page 34

NOW!
More Custom Hints
and Technical Tips

Merc Beats German Auto Union's International Record ... Page 20

. . . and Hop Up, of which the car's designer, Dean Batchelor, was the editor.

The flathead was bored and stroked up to 248 ci, and was configured to run mechanical fuel injection. For its 1952 Bonneville assault, the City of Burbank, California, sponsored the car. It really got the job done, setting a class record at an average 229.774 mph. It reached a speed of more than 235 mph on one of its one-way runs. But per Bonneville rules, to be an official record, the car must make two passes, one in each direction, up and down the track, and those runs are averaged; the second run, in the opposite direction of the first, must be made within one hour of the first run for the time to be sanctioned as official. Most impressive for a single engine car, although it wasn't long before multi-engine cars were exceeding this limit.

Isky himself was on hand for the runs and took several photos of the car on the salt, and the trophy presentations. Other sponsors included car dealer Bob Estes, Thalco Fiberglass, and General Petroleum. Although a very sophisticated design, the car was essentially home and hand-built by the team, for a cost of about $3,000 from 1951 to 1952.

The runs and record were considered somewhat of a home team victory for an all-American, Ford-powered car that was contesting records against the great prewar teams of Mercedes-Benz and Auto Union. The car was featured on the cover of the December 1952 issue of *Hop Up* magazine, of which designer Batchelor was editor, and the same month's issue of *Hot Rod*, wherein it was named Hot Rod of the Month.

Jazzy Jim Nelson

"Jazzy" Jim Nelson was, if nothing else, a drag racing innovator, as he was willing to try almost anything in terms of car design and layout to push the principles of physics and horsepower in search of a quicker quarter-mile run. One of his more notable efforts was his flathead Ford V-8-powered Fiat Topolino (which translates loosely from Italian as "little mouse").

Because of their diminutive size, many Americans called the compact Topolino a "Mickey Mouse Fiat." Obviously, the principle being pushed here was the notion of the car's weight-to-power ratio. The car didn't weigh much at all, and a race-built flathead V-8 certainly outpowered the Fiat's original 39-ci 4-cylinder engine, which was good for all of 16 hp.

Naturally, Isky supplied Nelson with cams and valvetrain gear, and the results were startling. The car's wheelbase was increased slightly in the name of high-speed stability. The little Italian coupe stood 59 inches tall and weighed 1,700 pounds, all mounted on a '34 Ford frame. It ran a 315-ci '49 Ford flathead (on fuel, not conventional gasoline), Edelbrock heads and manifold with four Stromberg 97s, and an Isky 404 cam, backed by a 1937 Cadillac transmission. On December 18, 1955, he clocked an unbelievable (to some) 9.10 elapsed time at 132.51 mph in the quarter-mile, really storming for an unsupercharged car. By the end of 1955, he had won an impressive 17 top eliminator titles, running against some of the fastest fuel dragsters in the country.

Nelson was, if nothing else, a loyalist, sticking with the venerable flathead Ford V-8 long after others felt its day was done. Subsequent to the Fiat, Nelson built a twin-engined dragster running two race-built flatheads mounted side to side in the chassis, with some rather complex driveline hardware to get the power from the two engines through a transmission, to the differential, and then to the ground. Ultimately, it wasn't as successful as the flathead Fiat, but it was very fast for its day and demonstrated that the little Ford V-8 could still compete and win races into the late 1950s.

Free Advertising

Isky remembers most but not all of the cars for which he gave promotional assistance and sponsorship and is surprised

"Jazzy" Jim Nelson understood the concept of weight-to-power ratio when he dreamed up this mighty, flathead-powered Fiat. The stiffened, underlying Ford frame has a much longer wheelbase than the tiny Topolino, which no doubt smoothed out the stability of Nelson's ride down the quarter. Progressive as he was, he was also a steadfast supporter of the Ford flathead, running them to great effect long after others thought their day was done.

This car competed handily with, and often beat, rail dragsters of the day. Of course, it ran an Isky 404 cam. (Photo Courtesy TEN: The Enthusiast Network Archive)

to occasionally stumble upon a car wearing his company name, decals, or stickers for which he has no recollection at all. "Sometimes somebody bought or just had one of my cams on hand, used it in their car, and put our name on it. We're happy about that, but would have likely given them the cam for free in exchange for a sponsorship agreement."

Two such examples are the gasser-style '55 Chevrolet coupe and the 1952 Henry J gasser owned by Debbie and Vic Young of Camarillo, California. The wicked primer-black '55 runs a 427-inch big-block Chevrolet, Jardine gasser headers, a straight axle front end, and an Isky cam. It is a very traditional, straightforward interpretation of a Chevy gas class dragster.

This flip-front Henry J runs an all-steel body and is highly evocative of so many gasser-type machines of the 1950s. Like Jim Nelson's Fiat, this car had a good weight-to-power ratio in its favor, compared to a heavier, full-size Ford, Chevy, or Chrysler. (Photo Courtesy Kirk Gerbracht)

Ed recalls that many car owners ran his cams and boasted about the fact, without him actually knowing about it or providing any sponsorship support. Nothing like free advertising! (Photo Courtesy Kirk Gerbracht)

The flip-front obviously makes engine access handy at the races and also opens up fender wells for easy header and exhaust routing. Gassers ran a variety of engines, with the small-block Chevy, later big-block Chevy, and Chrysler Hemi as the most popular. (Photo Courtesy Kirk Gerbracht)

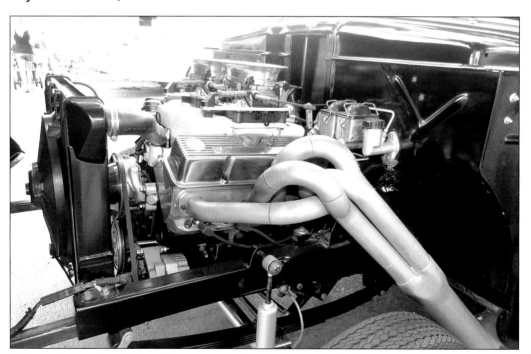

This particular "small-block" isn't so small anymore, punched out to 434 ci. With its side-by-side intake manifold, it sort of resembles the Chrysler cross-ram dual-quad design. (Photo Courtesy Kirk Gerbracht)

A classic Gasser, this shoebox Chevy represents a look that'll never get old, with a straight front axle, Torq Thrust wheels, a flip front without grille, a "home-fabbed tool-box" hood scoop, a big-block Chevy, and an Iskenderian Racing cam. (Photo Courtesy Kirk Gerbracht)

The nose sits a little high on this car, likely because that was the style back then, and also to aid in weight transfer upon launch. The nose of this car probably jumped another 6 inches when the tires really hooked up on a hard start. (Photo Courtesy Kirk Gerbracht)

The Youngs' Henry J boasts an all-steel body with a flipfront end and wears Mercedes-Benz Firemist Red paint. The engine is a 434-ci small-block Chevy V-8, running Edelbrock intake manifold and Edelbrock carbs, AFR aluminum heads, custom headers, and a Vertex electronic ignition, plus an Isky Roller Cam and Kit with roller rockers. A clean and very traditional interpretation of a gasser-style Henry J.

Ed inspected the Chevy in person and reviewed photos of the Henry J but didn't recall officially sponsoring either car, adding, "We put a lot of cams into a lot of Chevys and Henry Js over the years."

Big John Mazmanian

According to his official website biography, "Big John Mazmanian was born May 18, 1926, in Los Angeles. In junior

More classic Gas: an all-Willys run as Big John Mazmanian chooses to start off with the similar and equally notorious Stone, Woods & Cook Willys at the 1964 NHRA Winternationals at Pomona. (Photo Courtesy TEN: The Enthusiast Network Archive)

high school, he bought a 1930 Model A coupe for $25 and built his first car. He went through this car completely with the school auto shop teacher and turned it into a cool car. In high school, he had a 1939 Mercury with a chopped Carson top and DeSoto bumpers; it was painted black with a red interior.

After graduation, John attended college and earned a degree in mechanical engineering. At that time he had a 1932 highboy roadster that he raced on the streets; there weren't legal dragstrips anywhere yet. He also took the car to El Mirage dry lake after the police put a stop to the street racing. The roadster went 118 mph in early 1942.

After serving in World War II, John returned home and married his wife, Alice. He started running the family business and this took up most of his time, along with raising his family. Around 1957, John bought a 1957 Ford Fairlane "off the lot," which came with a supercharged 312. After using it as the family car on the weekdays, John doctored it up a bit and raced it on weekends.

John then stepped up to a 1961 Corvette, painted candy red, with fuel injection, 283 hp, 4-speed, and Posi-Traction. He ran it in C/Stock and then asked his nephew Rich Siroonian to drive it. They won the class honors at the Winternationals that year. John souped-up the 'Vette even more and had Bones Balough drive the candy-red car. By 1964, John had sold the 'Vette and bought a 1941 Willys coupe. He installed a 392 Chrysler Hemi in it and entered into the A/Gas class. In 1964, it ran 149 mph with a 9.77 ET.

In the late 1960s, the Willys was sold and John got ahold of an Austin. He painted it with his trademark candy-red paint. It had a chopped top and was called *The Football*. During his ownership of this car he teamed up with Junior Thompson, who put John's name on his own Austin and the cars traveled throughout the Midwest and Eastern United States. They were on a race circuit putting on great gasser shows at dragstrips across the United States and Canada.

The Austin was sold and John briefly entered the NHRA Funny Car ranks. He had a Barracuda with a Chrysler Hemi built but decided to retire in 1972. Big John still attended many major events and was inducted into the NHRA Hall of Fame in 1998. He was one of the honored Gasser Legends attending the Gateway Gasser Gathering in St. Louis, Missouri, in 1999. He, like Junior Thompson, said that the event was one of the best ever and he was glad to have been honored there.

Big John attended the Willys Reunion held at Thompson Raceway in Thompson, Ohio, during the weekend of June 1 and 2, 2002. He was one of the honored Gasser Legends attending, along with Junior Thompson, Ohio George, Bones Balough, and others. He died July 21, 2006. Isky recalls, "Big John ran my cams, as did Seto Postoian; at the beginning, it was a bit of an Armenian nepotism thing, but they both ran good and won using our stuff, so they both stayed with us a long time."

White Mist

The *White Mist* drag boat demonstrated that Isky cams ran not only on pavement, dirt, and the Bonneville salt, but on water as well. This particular iteration of *White Mist* was a Sanger flat bottom boat running an Isky-cammed Chrysler Hemi and reportedly made many race-winning runs at more than 117 mph, really storming in the late 1950s and early 1960s. This boat, based in Fresno, California, was most often driven by John Simas, and co-owned by Simas and Sanger Boats principal, Jack Davidson.

The blown 392 Hemi engines ran Isky 5-cycle cam and kit combinations, sometimes running straight alcohol and sometimes on an even more lethal nitro-methane fuel. The *White Mist* boat owned many drag racing boat records

Packing four Pontiac V-8s into a single streamliner required some real engineering, as did developing the drivetrain that could get all 3,000 hp to the salt. Isky liked and trusted that the young, handsome, and confident Mickey Thompson could get the job done at Bonneville, and recalls sponsoring him with about $6,000 worth of parts and seed money. Once again, Isky just knew which horse to hitch his promotional wagon to, and Thompson came away with great runs and a record. (Photo Courtesy TEN: The Enthusiast Network Archive)

Over time, there have been several Sanger drag boats named White Mist, and here's one of them, immaculately turned out, running a highly detailed early Chrysler Hemi and an Isky Racing cam, of course. (Photo Courtesy TEN: The Enthusiast Network Archive)

over time. As you can see, the boat's build quality, detailing, and prep were always immaculate.

Don Garlits

Isky met the soon-to-be-legendary Don Garlits around 1959, when he'd heard about the hot, young Tampa, Florida, drag racer who was somewhat of a big talker but also a very fast racer. He recalls "hearing, or reading, that Garlits went to a wrecking yard in 1958 or early 1959 to buy an Oldsmobile V-8 for a new dragster he was building. By the time he arrived, the engine had been sold, so the guy at the yard showed him a Chrysler Hemi that he had taken out of a wreck, and the pair decided that the Hemi, with its exotic-looking heads and valvecovers, looked like more of a racing engine than did the Olds, so Garlits bought that instead.

"Unbeknown to me, he called up and bought a cam from us . . . Of course, if we'd have known it was for a professional dragster, we'd have given him the cam for free, in exchange for sponsorship mention on his car.

"He was running really fast (180 mph and sometimes more) and winning a lot of races. And we started playing that up big in our advertisements in *Drag News* and such, and not long after, his car was renamed *Iskenderian Special*, which we really started playing up in our marketing. Of course, the other cam grinders were also looking for winning cars to make deals with so they had something to brag about too."

Garlits and Isky had a good relationship; Garlits won races running Isky parts, with the latter's name on his car, so it was race wins and good promotion. At some point, Isky recalls, "Garlits got a little grumpy, accusing Isky of supporting some of his West Coast teams with more money and/or goods than Garlits was receiving." So the two talked about an annual cash contract for sponsorship, which at the time may have been professional drag racing's

first financial sponsorship, that is, money over and above the providing of free parts and technical advice.

Isky and Garlits (who was not yet nicknamed Big Daddy) agreed to $1,000. Isky knew he'd tied himself to a winner and wanted an option for a second year as well, so they agreed to a $1,000 option for year two. About midway through the second year, Garlits received an offer of $5,000 per year from another cam company (Ray Giovannoni, a young upstart in the racing cam business). Isky of course objected and sought to protect his contract.

Isky took the issue up with his attorney, who attempted to establish what Isky's losses would be, to which Ed said, "There's really no way of knowing what our exact losses are because it's somewhat institutional advertising, and Ed didn't share in Garlits' winnings. So it would be difficult to quantify the losses in revenue from the lost promotion."

Isky was disappointed that he couldn't force Garlits' performance. So the lawyer and Garlits went to bat negotiating a settlement for Garlits' breach of the deal, and they settled on one year's sponsorship of $1,000. The attorney charged Isky $500 to negotiate the settlement, and another $500 for other work he'd done on Isky's behalf, so Ed ended up losing Garlits as name talent and the entire $1,000 settlement.

After some time, Garlits wasn't pleased with the Giovannoni cams and deal, and then switched to Crower cams. He wanted to come back to Ed about the time Chrysler brought out the new 426 "Street Hemi." Isky was one of the first cam companies to develop cams to get the new engine to really run in drag racing. Garlits felt a little bad that the previous deal with Isky soured over money, so he even offered to come back to Isky for no money, only in exchange for the latest and greatest equipment, which Isky agreed to supply.

Garlits ultimately stuck with Crower over another minor contract disagreement for which Isky elected to stand aside. These two racing icons shook hands, made

Altered-wheelbase dragsters with flopper front ends look a little out of proportion, but the Ramchargers used this technique, as did many other car builders, to get the driver location and weight balance just the way they wanted it, putting maximum weight over the rear end for best possible traction at launch.

Notice the Iskenderian Racing Cams sticker on the flopped-open front fender, just below the words "Original" and "Dodge." This is truly a moment from the heyday of early Mopar drag racing. (Photo Courtesy TEN: The Enthusiast Network Archive)

Bruce Geisler's Hanky Panky Special *Studebaker Lark* has notched more than 80 different records on the Bonneville salt. The Studes have always been popular LSR cars, given their compact size, relatively light weight, and aerodynamic-looking shape. Over time, it has run a variety of engines, from small-block Chevys to Buick V-6s.

On this day at Bonneville in 1968, it was running in the D Gas class, and its Chevy V-8 was equipped with an Isky Racing Cam, as you'll note from the list of credits painted on the fender just below the rear window. In more recent guise, it was powered by a Banks Engineering 258-inch small-block, running mechanical fuel injection, cranking out 670 hp at a lofty 9,500 rpm. Its likely more records will fall before Geisler and the Hanky Panky Special *retire from the salt. (Photo Courtesy TEN: The Enthusiast Network Archive)*

So many gasser class cars, particularly Willys, seemed to favor Isky cams. In 1961, Mike Marinoff decided to build a B/Gas Supercharged '41 Willys coupe. Once again, with Bill Reeves at controls, the car was one to be reckoned with, running elapsed times in the high-10s and speeds over 130 mph. Not only was it a terror on the Midwest gas coupe and sedan match race circuit, but the car also garnered another class win at the World Series in 1961. Left to right are Bill Reeves, Denny Sache, Dick Preeve, and Mike Marinoff. Notice Sache's Isky Racing Cams T-shirt. (Photo Courtesy Ed Iskenderian)

Jerry Kugel is a Bonneville veteran, having run several cars there over time, all fast and all beautifully turned out. This '32 roadster has run a variety of engines, among them a 260-inch small-block Ford, then a 289, and later a big-block mechanically fuel-injected 427.

This photo is from Bonneville 1967, where Kugel proudly wore his Iskenderian Cams Bonneville T-shirt and lettered his camshaft provider of preference on the side of the cowl, just aft of the engine compartment hood panels. The 427 pushed the little Deuce to a D/GR record of 205 mph, putting Kugel handily into Bonneville's vaunted 200 Mile an Hour Club. (Photo Courtesy TEN: The Enthusiast Network Archive)

big high-output engines ended up in the big, heavy cars rather than in any of the smaller models. And there was no formalized racing program. The group began to develop high-performance alternatives, powerplants, and programs that could compete with the hardware being assembled and raced at General Motors and Ford.

The group was loosely organized, but its epicenter was a nucleus of about a dozen men. The rules of play were simple: Any engineer or technician who wished to partake of Ramchargers' activities needed to do so off the Chrysler clock, meaning strictly on their own time. And the group had to be self-funding. They began meeting, almost in secret, about how high-performance cars could be culled from the Chrysler portfolio of bodies and chassis, and engines, both often highly modified for lighter weight and speed.

Several of the guys already raced Mopar products, so they became the foundation of the group's activities. Most of the cars raced in Stock and Super Stock classes, and altered-wheelbase classes. As time went along, they expanded to new Funny Car categories, and ultimately, rail dragsters.

Through a bit of reverse management, the group inspired or developed many great engines and models that became, almost in spite of themselves, Chrysler's muscle car and factory racing models. Isky Racing Cams wasn't the sole provider of camshafts and valve gear for the Ramchargers, but it equipped many of the cars because Isky had such great success configuring and producing cams for the early- and later-generation Hemis, 413s, 426 wedge engines, and the big 440.

Look at enough old photos of Ramcharger cars at the strip and you'll see a variety of camshaft sponsor stickers on them. But for a while in the early and mid-1960s, Isky provided cams for many of the cars and the Ramchargers returned the favor with countless big race wins and large lettering on the sides of its cars. Isky remembers them as "great guys, and a serious bunch of racers."

Mickey Thompson

Ed Iskenderian clearly remembers the day that a handsome, somewhat brash young racer and hot rodder named Mickey Thompson walked into his shop, asking for camshafts, valvetrain gear, and financial support for a new streamliner he was building for Bonneville in 1960. His goal, which he was quite sure he could attain, was to break the 400-mph record. Thompson's radical new streamliner was to be named *Challenger I* and would be powered by four Pontiac V-8 engines.

Thompson himself was the car owner/builder and planned to drive the car to the land speed record. Isky found Thompson to be well-spoken, confident, even a little cocky, but knowledgeable about the engineering principles of his car. He invited Isky to his shop to see the car under construction and validate his ideas.

Isky liked Thompson and the concept of the car; he understood that his parts helping a 400-mph record setter held great promotional appeal. He talked Thompson's sponsorship request over with his friend Vic Edelbrock, who wasn't as immediately impressed. Vic told Isky, "He didn't really know if Thompson was for real because he'd never bought a single part from Edelbrock, nor had he ever requested any sponsorship or parts from him."

Isky understood that there was some risk in the deal with the possibilities that Thompson would never actually build and run the car, or that he would make the runs but fall short of the records he was shooting for. Yet in spite of some concerns over the magnitude of the goal, the inexperience of its protagonist, and the reservations voiced by the savvy and experienced Edelbrock, Isky liked Thompson and wanted to be part of the effort.

He also recalled that, "It was clear that Mickey had some support from General Motors, since I think they gave him the Pontiac engines. Mickey, of course, needed at least four cams for the engines and lots of associated valvetrain components, plus

If Thompson were nervous, you wouldn't know it from this pre-record run photo. He actually seems to be dozing. Even though Thompson was usually an animated man, he was said to be ultra cool at the wheel. (Photo Courtesy TEN: The Enthusiast Network Archive)

Thompson and team, post-run, wave the checkered flag and gather to verify the results and likely share a few good handshakes and some backslapping. Thompson is in the dark pants with his back to the camera. (Photo Courtesy TEN: The Enthusiast Network Archive)

Job done. The MT Racing team and Challenger I take a well-deserved bow and photo op after the successful Bonneville runs in 1960. Note the black streaks from the side outlet exhaust systems on the flanks of the car. (Photo Courtesy TEN: The Enthusiast Network Archive)

It was common for the makers of racing parts and other aftermarket goodies to give their customers little tin or brass "timing plaques" that could be engraved with the specs of their car, cam, the results of their run, or whatever. This is Isky's plate, incorporating acknowledgment of the company's participation in Mickey Thompson's historic assault on Bonneville in 1960 in Challenger I. (Photo Courtesy Ed Iskenderian)

some expense money, so I just decided to go for it."

Isky hitched his caboose to a fast train, and it was truly ready to rock when its moment in the Utah sun came on September 9, 1960, as the 32-cylinder, supercharged, Pontiac-powered *Challenger I* thundered its way across the salt with a best one-way time of 406.6 mph. The 7,000-pound, 3,000-hp *Challenger* was sponsored by Iskenderian Racing Cams, Champion Spark Plugs, Mobil Oil, Goodyear Tire and Rubber, and Cragar.

Isky was so pleased with this accomplishment that he elected to have the event commemorated on the small metal "timing plaques" that he gave out to racing customers that ran and won with his products. The plaque that contains a stylized illustration of an Isky camshaft and the Challenger I in profile. It reads, "This car is equipped with an Iskenderian Racing Cam – the World's Fastest." A small data panel allowed the driver to boast about the specs of the cam, and noted "Mickey Thompson's Challenger I the fastest car in the World, [a true statement at the time] Bonneville Utah, 1960. 406.6 MPH." Isky remains tremendously proud of his role in Thompson's accomplishments of "an American car, with an American driver, American engines, on American soil, running at over 400 mph."

Goldenrod

As great as Mickey Thompson's accomplishments were with *Challenger I*, he wasn't by any measure the only American effort to assault various definitions and classes of the land speed record. There have been many, powered by a variety of rockets and jet engines, but there was one more particularly historic wheel-driven effort using piston engine power. That was the Summers brothers' *Goldenrod*.

Bill and Bob Summers were based in Ontario, California, just an hour or so northeast of Isky's Inglewood, California, shop. Bob was the primary driver. *Goldenrod* was only similar to Thompson's *Challenger I* in being powered by four American V-8 engines and running Isky racing cams. In this case, however, the engines were fuel-injected Chrysler Hemi V-8s instead of Pontiacs.

The Summers salt assault came just five years after Thompson's, and the result was a world record two-way average of 409.277 mph on November 12, 1965, besting Thompson by only a few MPH but backing it up with a two-way run, required to earn official international recognition of the speed as a record. Ed Iskenderian is equally proud of being a part of both efforts.

Goldenrod held the record it earned from 1965 to 1991. It was purchased by

This great auto show photo gives you an idea of how long the Summers Brothers' Goldenrod LSR car really is; it takes a lot of wheelbase to pack in four Chrysler Hemis, a driver, and a drivetrain. Perhaps in further celebration of the car's records and "gold medal" performance is the appearance of Linda Vaughn, the irrepressible Miss Hurst Golden Shifter, at this event. Just look for the woman with the bouffant of long blonde hair just inside the ropes near the front of the car. (Photo Courtesy TEN: The Enthusiast Network Archive)

The Henry Ford [museum] in Dearborn in 2002, and subsequently restored by former magazine editor John Baechtel and long-time Bonneville competitor Mike Cook. It will live out its life in retirement on public display at the Henry Ford.

The Indy 500

Ed speaks with pride about the three instances when he was specifically involved in providing cams for an Indianapolis 500 effort. They were in 1962, 1980, and 1981. Recall that in the early 1960s, the mid/rear engine racer was beginning to replace the older front engine roadsters that competed in the USAC champ car series and at the Speedway. The first rear engine car to run at Indy did so in 1961, and by 1963 there were several, chief among them the Lotus team. The slender, cigar-shaped Lotus racers were powered by Ford's new lightweight, small-block Fairlane V-8 that went on to power millions of Mustangs and countless other Fords over the next several decades.

Isky recalls that someone from Lotus contacted him asking him to make a cam that would give the lightweight British machines good passing and top-end power. Ed provided the cam and a set of premium high-RPM valvetrain components to be used in Jimmy Clark's green and yellow Lotus. Clark nearly won the race, coming home second in a controversial run to the finish with ultimate winner Parnelli

Ed attended Indy several times. It's doubtful that he has ever been so pleased with a second-place finish, as he was when Jim Clark, in his beautiful rear-engine Ford-powered Lotus, finished a hard-earned runner-up to Parnelli Jones, in the historic 1963 Indianapolis 500. Even though Indy-style racing wasn't his normal target market, he was obviously thrilled to see his logo near the front of the Big Race. Ed also provided the cams for the 1980 race-winning Cosworth Chaparral of Johnny Rutherford. (Photo Courtesy Ford Motosport Archive)

Jones in J. C. Agajanian's front-engined, Offenhauser-powered roadster, nicknamed *Ol' Calhoun*. Jones seemed to be in command of the race, but Clark was wicked fast and reeling him in.

Jones's Watson roadster was equipped with an external oil tank mounted just on the outside of the bodywork next to the drive. It developed a crack and was leaking oil onto Jones's left rear tire and blowing oil onto the track and the cars behind him, so the race stewards contemplated giving Jones the black flag for creating a potentially unsafe condition. That, of course, would have meant that the race outcome would have been decided by a technicality, not on the track, not what anyone really wanted.

While car owner Agajanian lobbied his case to the officials, the oil leak had emptied the tank to below the level of the crack. So the leaking stopped. After much heated trackside discussion, the officials elected to allow Jones to continue and let things sort themselves out. If the leak had drained the tank of enough oil for the Offy to survive, it would blow up and put Jones out of the race, in a bit of natural selection. If Clark otherwise had enough speed to catch Jones and run him down, the cards would fall where they may, but it appeared the leak was no longer a hazard to the cars behind Jones. They let it be for the remaining handful of laps, the oil-starved Offenhauser somehow kept on churning, and Jones took his only Indy 500 win, the Isky-cammed Lotus of Jim Clark finishing a hard-earned second place. Isky was very proud of this occasion and featured it in his upcoming advertisements.

Isky was again a camshaft provider in 1980, when Jim Hall prepared to run a Cosworth-powered Chaparral for two-time winner Johnny Rutherford. Isky recalls that Hall's engine builder procured a quartet of unfinished cams from Cosworth, and the Isky cam team designed lobe profiles for the high-revving, turbocharged V-8, and ground the cams. Rutherford in his *Yellow Submarine* Chaparral chassis won the race going away, giving Isky Racing Cams a long-deserved Indy 500 victory.

Dan Gurney's All American Eagles

Another Indy racing involvement that Isky is very proud of is having supplied cams for several years to Dan Gurney's All American Racers. Isky has great admiration for Gurney, as both began their automotive involvement as kids playing with hot rods at the dry lakes and Bonneville. Even as turbocharged Cosworth and Ford DOHC V-8s battled with the trusty old Offenhauser for Indy racing supremacy, Gurney felt there was much value and potential left to be found in naturally aspirated, overhead valve V-8 "stock-block" engines, primarily the small-block Ford and small-block Chevrolet V-8s.

Among the AAR Eagle Indy cars Gurney is most proud of is the Pepsi Challenger Eagle of the early 1980s. The car was sponsored by Pepsi at the time, and one of its advertising slogans was to "take the Pepsi Challenge [versus Coke, of course] so its Indy car was logically named Challenger. It was a highly innovative car aerodynamically and very attractive from any angle.

It ran side pods that fared up and over the rear wheels a bit (not unlike today's Indy car bodywork) and ran an utterly unique dual-rear-wing design; the lower rear wing was a swoopy part of the car's bodywork, while another more traditional wing sat farther up in the air stream. The car was designed and built entirely in-house by All American Racers in Santa Ana, California.

Gurney and the AAR team felt the car needed an innovative powerplant to match its innovative chassis and bodywork, so they developed a small-block Chevrolet V-8 from scratch to run, in addition to the occasional use of the popular and successful Cosworth DFX. The engine, still naturally aspirated with overhead valves, was all aluminum and based on a

Donovan engine block and alloy heads. It displaced the series mandated maximum of 355 ci and cranked out around 650 hp.

Isky Racing Cams provided the camshafts for this AAR-built engine, and Ed recalls one particular conversation with Gurney about cylinder head and combustion chamber design: "Dan Gurney is smart. And he really understands engines. One time we were talking about cylinder heads and spark plug and fuel-injector design and locations, and we really got into the subject and talked about it for hours. Then they made some minor changes to the combustion chamber design on this car and it picked up all kinds of horsepower."

The innovative Pepsi *Challenger* was successful, but only to the extent that the CART series rule makers would let it be. AAR's principal drivers were Mike Mosley and Geoff Brabham. The car never won Indy but was competitive and ran well. In one rather astounding accomplishment, Mosley started the 1981 Milwaukee CART race from the last row because he missed formal qualifying. Mosley stormed his way through the field from last place to victory lane, and if the race would have been longer, he likely could have lapped the entire field on his way to this historic last to first-place victory. The car was soon banned by the CART officials for being too different and allegedly not being in compliance with the spirit and letter of the rules.

Even so, Isky can take pride in his company's participation in the top ranks of Indy car racing, by helping power the innovative AAR Pepsi Challenger to an impressive race win on the Milwaukee Mile, a hard-earned second place in the 1962 Indy 500, and a big win at Indy in 1980.

One look at the ultra-innovative AAR Pepsi Challenger, right, compared with the much more conventional AAR Indy Car just a few years older (left) shows that Challenger was something very special and different. The aerodynamic philosophies of the two designs are obviously and markedly different. AAR ran its Donovan-based small-block Chevy V-8 design for several seasons in the early 1980s (although for one of those seasons it was badged as a Buick), and they all ran Isky cams.

Chapter 6

BEYOND 1960 AND ISKY TODAY

The Isky Racing Cam generations. Ed, at left, and his sons Richard, Ron, and Timothy hanging out and around with "Number-1," Isky's original Norton grinder, which still takes pride of place on the shop floor. Even though it dates from the 1930s, it still has enough juice to grind out a cam once in a while. (Photo Courtesy Mel Stone)

At the dawn of the 1950s, Isky Racing Cams as a business was little more than a blacksmith shop that made automotive parts. During the ensuing decade, the industry grew tremendously. Isky's business grew up along with it and by 1960 it was the dominant force in the performance and racing cam–grinding industry. Ed earned his stripes not only as an innovator whose products worked well, but also as a voice for the growth and professionalizing of the business. Not to mention his supreme marketing and promotional skills, from pit crew T-shirts advertising his business, to the sponsorship and technical involvement with several important land speed record efforts at Bonneville, to the same with the biggest names in drag racing.

Success in the NHRA

The depth to which Isky had made an impact in drag racing was best demonstrated at the NHRA Nationals event in Indianapolis, Indiana, in 1962. The Indy Nationals is one of the largest and most hotly contested drag racing meets on the NHRA annual championship calendar. In 1962, Isky racing cams powered 27 first-place award winners.

It was a huge and multifaceted domination of the meet, with Isky-equipped cars winning a wide variety of classes, from

One of Ed's proudest accomplishments was when Isky Racing Cams products powered 27 individual class winners at the 1962 NHRA Indy Nationals. (Photo Courtesy Ed Iskenderian)

This may look like a pile of scrap metal, but it tells a great and important story. In Ed's earliest days of building and racing Ford flathead V-8s, nobody really knew exactly how thick the walls of the in-block intake and exhaust ports were, which of course impacted how much they could be ported, polished, or otherwise ground and opened in the search for more airflow.

Ed didn't have easy access to the sonic-testing technology now used by engine builders and racing teams to find the thickest or thinnest parts of a block, cylinder head, or intake manifold, so he sacrificed a flathead engine block in the pursuit of this information by cutting the areas around the ports into small pieces to locate the thick or thin parts of the casting. This information is critical, because if you grind or port these areas too thin, they are susceptible to cracking or perhaps even grinding into a cylinder wall or cooling jacket, which are surefire direct flights to future engine failure.

Ed has kept this wired-together pile of engine block casting bits for decades, as a quiet reminder of the innovation that was needed to learn the game back in the day.

production-bodied stock categories to Top Eliminator, the overall top class winner of the event. Isky was so pleased with this accomplishment that he had special posters made up showing a photo of each winning car, its driver, and the class trophy. In addition, each winning driver received from Isky a red varsity-style racing jacket, embroidered in red, white, blue, and gold on the back with "1962 NHRA Nationals Class Champion, Iskenderian Cam Equipped."

The Top Eliminator winning car was the *Mickey Thompson Special* (entered by the same Mickey Thompson that Ed sponsored at Bonneville in 1960) and driven by a young Jack Chrisman. The car was powered by a supercharged Pontiac engine running experimental Hemi-style heads.

Models and Kits

It was about this time that the performance aftermarket really began to mature as an industry. Ed's mind, always in search of the next promotional tool or opportunity, grew curious about how plastic model kit producers decided what stickers and decals to include in each model kit. He remembers looking at some AMT model kits of cars he knew and paid particular attention to the little page of decals included in the box and what companies were represented there and which were not.

Naturally he wanted his Isky Racing Cams stickers and logos to be represented.

So he consulted an attorney that specialized in trademarks and brands about how he could get his company onto those little decals pages. He was also emphatic about the fact that he wasn't looking for money from the model kit builders, only the promotional value of kids building plastic model cars and putting his name on the side. His hope was that when these kids grew up and bought full-size cars of their own that they would remember Isky Racing Cams from their model cars, and maybe want to purchase the real thing.

As with most things he pursued, Isky was successful in this endeavor, and after some effort, some of the model kit makers began to include Isky's company logo on their decals pages. In discussions about the performance aftermarket with this attorney, the latter said, "You guys should really organize yourselves." Isky didn't understand what he meant, so he dug a little deeper, and the attorney suggested that they form a trade association as a forum for information, best practices exchange, the sharing of ideas on how to do business, and for legislative representation.

SEMA

It all began in 1963 when a group of small manufacturers who were suppliers of performance equipment for early hot rods organized their fledgling industry and called it Speed Equipment Manufacturers Association (SEMA). The mission was practical and straightforward: develop

As time went along, the brand name became shorter and shorter, all the better to fit on T-shirts, decals, jacket patches, and stickers. The red, white, and blue livery is no accident; Isky is a proud American and his company, like its products, are made in the United States. (Photo Courtesy Ed Iskenderian)

This is one of Ed's early tradeshow booths The gent in the photo is ad guy Ed Elliott, who helped a small group of aftermarket speed parts makers organize to form SEMA. This small booth is casual and homey compared to the multi-thousand-square-foot booths and displays that larger companies now employ at SEMA. Today's SEMA show covers hundreds of thousands of square feet, housing thousands of booths and displays, and 95-year-old Ed still attends and supports the organization he helped found.

I was originally advised that this photo had been taken at an early SEMA show, but the watercraft in all the photos in the booth likely indicate otherwise. (Photo Courtesy TEN: The Enthusiast Network Archive)

An august crowd in the world of automotive aftermarket and publishing: from left are Isky, publishing magnate Robert E. Petersen, former Hot Rod editor Ray Brock, and competing publisher Noel Carpenter. (Photo Courtesy TEN: The Enthusiast Network Archive)

Isky is a big fan of and was a friend of the late Phil Weiand, who was partially paralyzed in a public road speed test accident at the wheel of his Model T when he was still a teen. Phil's main game was high-performance intake manifolds, although he later produced blower drives, valvecovers, and many other go-fast and dress-up parts. Even though he was in a wheelchair for most of his adult life, Phil went on to build and run a successful speed parts business. His first shop was in his mother's garage, but he became one of the early and major players in the aftermarket performance game. (Photo Courtesy TEN: The Enthusiast Network Archive)

Hail to the (SEMA) Chief, as SEMA president Ed Iskenderian cuts a rug with his wife, Alice. Previous to this, Ed didn't know how to dance and didn't want to look stupid if he ever got hauled out onto a dance floor, so he bit the macho bullet and took dancing lessons. Here, he's having fun at an early SEMA show banquet. (Photo Courtesy TEN: The Enthusiast Network Archive)

uniform standards for certain products used in motorsports competition; promote the industry as a supplier to consumers involved in constructive activities of recreational and hobbyist value; develop programs to encourage improved business practices among member companies; and hold regular meetings to achieve unity as a business organization. In those days, all of the members were founders of companies that produced speed equipment exclusively (hence, the organization's title).

The group that ultimately banded together to found SEMA in 1963 is in itself a small "who's who" of the performance industry. SEMA's founding fathers are Louis Senter, Ansen Automotive Engineering; Bob Spar, B & M Automotive; Roy Richter, Cragar Industries; Else Lohn, Eelco Manufacturing & Supply; John Bartlett, Grant Industries; Ed Iskenderian, Isky Racing Cams; Don Alderson, Milodon Engineering; Dean Moon, Moon Equipment; Paul Schiefer, Schiefer Manufacturing; Willie Garner, Trans Dapt; Harry Weber, Weber Speed Equipment; Phil Weiand, Weiand Power & Racing; and Dempsey Wilson, Dempsey Wilson Racing cams.

Ed recalls missing the meeting when the group chose officers, so they elected him president in 1963. He was also reelected president in 1964. Although the group was initially formed around companies that produced speed equipment only, they felt that banding together with other types of aftermarket equipment makers was ultimately better for everyone, on the grounds of strength in numbers. So they later welcomed as members companies producing a much wider variety of products, including wheels, paint, tires, lighting, and the kaleidoscope of aftermarket products for motorsports, cars, and trucks.

In recognition of this wider scope of its membership, and perhaps in the interests of presenting a slightly more friendly persona, the group changed its name from Speed Equipment to Specialty Equipment Market Association.

Isky was inducted into the SEMA Hall of Fame in 1978 and continues to be a major supporter of the organization, and its world famous annual SEMA trade show held each fall in Las Vegas. He's particularly proud of that recognition, in addition to being inducted into Chevrolet's Legends of Performance Hall of Fame in 1986. As you can imagine, he's been lauded with countless recognitions and awards throughout his long life and career. Another high point was being presented with the Robert E. Petersen Lifetime Achievement Award at the 2012 Hot Rod and Restoration Trade Show.

He's most recently been lauded with the Justice Brothers' Shav Glick award; Glick was the *Los Angeles Times'* legendary motorsports writer, and Justice Brothers presents this award annually for contributions to the world of racing. Past winners include Dan Gurney, Phil Hill, Jeff Gordon, Carroll Shelby, and Don Prudhomme.

On the Move Again

When Isky Racing Cams moved to Inglewood, California, Ed figured it would be large enough to last the company for decades to come. Even at approximately 20,000 square feet, it just wasn't enough. But the property came with some extra land to one side, so Ed began to explore expanding his building. After analyzing the costs to prepare the lot for the construction, plus building costs, it was clear that it was less costly to move than to expand.

So he began the search for a new location, which made financial sense but was also a bitter pill because he'd built the Inglewood location from the ground up, and it was a high-quality building. Regardless, he found an industrial building at the northeast corner of Broadway and Alondra Boulevards in nearby Gardena. It was a former machine shop that had gone out of business, sitting on about two acres of land. It was already equipped with a 30,000-square-foot office and shop building.

An aerial shot of Isky Racing Cams current Gardena location, clearly shows its four main buildings, plus "Isky's private junkyard" at the top of the photo, which, long ago, was the employee parking lot. (Photo Courtesy Ed Iskenderian)

Ed never failed to get a photo of his legendary hot rod in front of each of his new shops. This is the current Gardena, California, location when it opened in the mid-1960s. (Photo Courtesy TEN: The Enthusiast Network Archive)

This is the south-facing side of Isky's main building. The fact that the "K" is missing its blue plastic material is a testament to today's casual nature of the facility. (Photo Courtesy Mel Stone)

As the 1950s became the 1960s, Ed already recognized that little engines could go fast, and they needed hot cams too. Among Isky's early hits for small engines was for the venerable air-cooled 4-cylinder Volkswagen engine, popular for the burgeoning dune buggy market, the expansion of off-roading, street performance, and also drag racing VWs. (Photo Courtesy TEN: The Enthusiast Network Archive)

The building would suit his needs, allow room for future expansion, and the terms were good: 10 percent down with the balance payable at 6-percent interest. It was located near the freeway in a largely industrial area, close to his home, and not far from where some of his friends owned businesses. Ed's old shop sold easily and quickly, so he picked up and moved Isky Racing Cams to its current and likely permanent location in Gardena. Over time, they've added several additional metal buildings, giving them about 75,000 square feet under roof.

The 1960s was a decade of continued growth for the company. Product lines were added, including the expansion of the use of roller camshafts, roller rocker assemblies, adjustable pushrods, heavy-duty valvesprings, and more. What used to be called the "cam and kit" became more commonly known as the "cam and coordinated assembly." Fewer customers came in for just a camshaft, and more and more walked away with valvesprings, rockers, lifters, and pushrods.

This gave way to more and more creative names for these products: Tool Room Racing Valve Springs, Red-Zone Roller Lifters, EZ-Roll Lifters, Accelerator Maximum Roller Cams, to name a few. The valvespring aspect of the business really increased, with a variety of heavy-duty single, double, and even triple valvespring combinations offered for extreme use.

Another area of expansion was the development and offering of high-performance cams and valvetrain gear for more and more engines. Even though Isky Racing Cams is an absolutely all-American company, Ed recognized good market potential in offering cams for certain imported cars as they became ever more popular during the 1960s and early 1970s.

One particularly popular option was for the Volkswagen flat-4. The VW's stock cam is particularly conservative, aimed primarily at fuel economy and a smooth idle. Lots of power was to be found in the tiny air-cooled engine with a more aggressive cam profile, with surprisingly little negative impact on fuel economy; when an engine runs more efficiently, it puts out better power and can still deliver good fuel mileage. Isky cams are now available for Toyota, Nissan, and Honda engines, as well as other popular imports such as the BMC A-series engine, found under the hood of countless MGs, and Minis.

All in the Family

Isky claims to be one of the first high-performance companies to employ computers to aid in the design of camshaft profiles; this at a time when only defense contractors, the military, NASA, and the government commonly used computer-aided design. Sons Richard, Ron, and Timothy all grew up in the business, and today have vital roles in the company's leadership. Ed is still the primary overseer, while Richard is company president and Ron is primarily involved in developing new cam profiles and other products.

Together, the two older sons have come to market with hundreds of new or revised cam profiles. Tim has formed his own sub-brand, Tim Iskenderian Cams, and although he still works for "big Isky," he also has developed and produces a line of high-performance cams for small-bore single- and 2-cylinder engines, such as you might find in all-terrain vehicles and racing karts. Imagine a single-cylinder lawnmower-style engine that can push a small tube-framed minibike to more than 100 mph.

It is indeed a family affair. Isky's younger brother Ben also worked at the company from 1952 to 1977, a nice round 25-year career in the cam business. He started out on the line, working a cam grinder, then advanced to more supervisor and management roles. Today, Ben says that he enjoys and celebrates his brother's success and, equally, his years with the company. He only wishes he'd have gotten out to more of the races that the company supported. By spending most of his time

Other Voices

Paul Pfaff (pronounced "fahf") is a retired fire captain, hot rodder, racer, and engine builder who built one of the most capable and legendary racing-engine building shops in the business. He has known Ed Iskenderian for decades and used a variety of his products in his own and customer engines through the years. "Some people accuse Ed of being more of a promoter than an innovator, but that's not true," notes Pfaff. "There's no question that Ed is a character, and a first-rate marketer, but his stuff works. I've run a bunch of his cams in small-block and big-block Chevys, and they run great. I also ran his cam in my flathead hot rod way back when, and it worked when nobody else's stuff did. The Isky 404 is still the best flathead cam ever, in my opinion.

"Remember, Ed got started when cam grinding was more of a black art than a science, and he figured out a lot of stuff and made it work. I've also had a lot of good luck with Crane cams; two legendary names, Isky and Crane, and both are the real deal as far as I'm concerned."

Robert Jung and Kurtis Hooker have both worked most of their adult lives at Edelbrock, primarily in product development, testing, and R & D. They've both spent countless days and hours dyno testing a wide variety of engine components, those made by Edelbrock and others. Hooker quips that, "Every story you've ever heard about Isky is probably true, the good, the bad, and the ugly. Isky Racing Cams has always produced solid parts. The stuff is top quality."

Jung added to that thought with a story about running one of Vic Edelbrock's boat engines, which broke a lifter during the run. "All the valve gear was Ed's stuff. He was very concerned about what went wrong. We were still tearing the engine down when, a few minutes later, Ed showed up knocking at the back door, wanting to see the lifter and any other associated parts that broke or may have caused the damage. We got to the broken part and Ed said he'd take it back to the shop so he could figure out for sure what went wrong and that he'd stand behind it."

Hooker took up the discussion about Ed's prowess as innovator versus promoter: "Ed loves the angle of marketing, not only for his company, but for racing and for the aftermarket parts industry, which is part of the reason he was such a big force in the formation of SEMA."

Jung continues: "And Ed's always out there among the people. Whether it's making a speech or signing autographs, Ed is out there with the racers and enthusiasts. Doesn't matter if it's the Grand National Roadster Show or an open house at some guy's shop, Ed is there, representing his company and our industry. And people just love him.

"I don't think Isky Racing Cams is the innovation leader it used to be; the stuff, while very good and solid, is a little more conservative than some of the others. But Ed's energy and enthusiasm is endless. He certainly supports big-time pro racers, but he's really there

Engine builder extraordinaire Paul Pfaff has been in the game a long time. He has had several business partners and numerous locations prior to the large, world-class engine shop he ultimately ended up with in Huntington Beach, California. This early 1960s ad describes the variety of services Pfaff & Sowins offered. Pfaff speaks highly of Crane and Isky cams.

Kurtis Hooker, left, has worked for Edelbrock for nearly 50 years, and Robert Jung, right, for more than 30, demonstrating that two-way loyalty goes a long way in their business. Running the dynamometer testing rooms is among their responsibilities as R & D chiefs for the company.

Here they work in one of the dyno "cells" setting up a Ford engine for power testing. Both have known Isky for decades, speak warmly of him, appreciate Ed's interest in his customers' satisfaction, the fact that Isky Racing Cams parts work and are of good quality.

Edelbrock now produces its own camshafts, which are designed to work in concert with its coordinated valvetrain components and the complete engines the company sells.

Writer, racer, and TV personality Steve Magnante is cranking up a Chrysler 426 Ramcharger engine for a dyno test. As a rookie feature writer at Hot Rod, he was sent to cover a story at Isky's and will never forget the experience. His only complaint about this photo is that he wasn't wearing his Isky Racing Cams T-shirt that day. (Photo Courtesy Steve Magnante)

for the little-guy racers too, bracket racers, 'run what you brung' racers, whatever. The 'little-guy' racer is just as important to him as Don Garlits. And *everybody* knows Isky.

"And I've always admired his ability to share credit when giving credit is due. He'll always acknowledge anyone who helped him along the way, or share credit with someone at his shop who came up with something good."

Steve Magnante is a former technical editor of *Hot Rod* and is now a well-known television commentator, freelance writer, and enthusiast drag racer who has always enjoyed his interactions with Isky. Here's the story of his first meet-up with The Camfather: "I was a recent hire at *Hot Rod* when then-editor Ro McGonegal assigned me to visit Isky to do a story about his Spintron cam and valvetrain dyno endurance and test simulator.

"The year was 1998 or so and Ro mentioned that I'd probably meet Ed Iskenderian during my visit. As a kid, I'd read all about Ed Iskenderian in all the magazines before I became a *Hot Rod* staffer (1997 to 2004) and knew he was one of the pioneers of the Southern California speed equipment scene. So the idea of meeting a legend was exciting. As I mentioned, my upcoming visit to other Petersen Publishing staffers who'd already been to Isky (it was a rite of passage for any tech editor), a recurring theme was the supposed mountains of books, magazines, catalogs, and other paper clutter that was said to surround Ed's desk and office work station.

"Sure enough, when I entered the main building on the Isky campus, Ed was seated at his desk, but some of the piles of literature obscured him from view. It wasn't a messy scene; in fact, I had the feeling I could have pulled out a random item (like a playing

Wherever he goes, Isky is a star. On this particular day, while enjoying lunch with his pals, a documentary TV crew was shadowing him for a tour around his shop and a typical day in his life. Seated from left: lifelong pal John Athan, Ed (center), and Nick Arias Jr. You may recognize Nick's name primarily for the manufacture of high-performance pistons that are particularly successful in racing. John joins the group only once a week or so, but Nick has lunch with Isky nearly every day.

card from a deck) and he'd blow off the dust and know instantly what it was and why he kept it. Minutes after a brief introduction, my guide led me to the dyno room where the Spintron awaited. Essentially an engine dyno in reverse, it used a massive electric motor connected to the test engine's crankshaft. There were no pistons or connecting rods in the engine and no combustion took place. Rather, the goal was to observe the motion of the camshaft, timing set, lifters, push rods, rocker arms, valvesprings, and other related parts to evaluate their performance and durability. After all, Isky's business was (and is) centered on the engine's valvetrain.

"What struck me that day (besides Ed's 4-foot-tall stacks of literature) was how much noise is generated by an engine's valvetrain. The test engine was a Chevy small-block. With the huge electric motor spinning its crankshaft at 7,000 rpm, the sound generated was nearly indistinguishable from a self-powered engine on a normal dyno. It was loud! The only thing missing was the guttural roar of combustion and the stifling heat. As I stood in awe, Ed entered the room to check our progress. He stayed briefly, and the noise prevented much discussion. The Spintron was simulating a road course, complete with the frequent RPM cycles of up-and-down shifting in the corners.

"By the end of the day, I had my story for *Hot Rod*, and I like to think that our four-page exposé helped launch Isky's (then brand new) Gold Stripe Tool Room valvespring campaign, 16 of which were on that passive test engine humming and clattering away aboard the Isky Spintron that day."

Dave McClelland hails from the South and worked as a professional drag racing announcer and event emcee for some five decades. He'd been doing some work as a local TV and radio newscaster, so had the ability to string sentences together, and he possesses a clear booming baritone voice, so he was a natural. In the early 1960s he joined the NHRA's official broadcasting staff and spent the next several decades calling some of the most important drag racing matchups of all time.

In the earliest days he only knew Isky by name and reputation. Some years later, he was invited to act as emcee at Ed's 90th birthday party. The pair have come in contact many times since, and McClelland categorizes Isky as "a most remarkable individual. He was an early innovator in the speed parts business, and it's amazing he's still at it 70 years later. Ed was never afraid to experiment or try something new in the cam and valvetrain business, and more often than not, he was right, and what he tried usually worked.

"He's also a superb businessman, never trying to cut quality over price, yet never gouging his customer either; high-quality stuff at a fair price. And he's wonderful with people and so much a fan favorite. I've seen him at car shows and drag racing events, and everyone wants to shake his hand, tell him a story, get an autograph, and have a photo taken with him. And even when it gets a little hectic, he's always patient and under control. An absolute icon of our industry."

Ed Justice Jr. is a longtime motorsports photographer and current president of engine and fuel additive maker Justice Brothers, which has sponsored many racing efforts of all stripes, including several Indy 500 drivers and teams. He speaks about Ed Iskenderian with great respect, bordering on reverence: "Isky, grinding cams on his homebuilt cam-grinding machine in the back of John Athan's tool and die shop, working on a dirt floor, and his little Model T hot rod running up at the dry lakes, to me is the birth of hot rodding as we know it. If a carmaker came out with a new engine, it wasn't out five minutes before Isky profiled and ground up cams for it.

"The founding president of SEMA, he and just a few other guys are the genesis of modern hot rodding. He knew everybody in the business, because he was there, and they all knew him. A legend, and one of the nicest guys you'll ever meet."

Ed and younger brother Ben couldn't look more alike. Their roundish heads, stocky builds, and barrel chests ensure that. Ben and his brother meet for lunch often, and Ben often visits the shop to walk the production floor and see what's happening. Here, the Isky brothers inspect a group of Buick V-6 cams in the mid-production process.

at the shop, he got to meet only a few of the more prominent drivers the company supported or sponsored. Of course, disgruntled customers seemed to end up at his office door to resolve any equipment problems that may have arisen.

Now in his early 80s, Ben is fully retired and often joins his brother and friends for lunch to talk cars, cams, and old times. He's intelligent, sharp, and well-spoken.

Isky Racing Cams employs about 50 technicians and specialists, many of whom joined the company as their first job and have remained there for decades.

Even though no longer the volume leader in the high-performance cam business, Isky Racing Cams is still a viable and highly active player in the game. Ed doesn't believe that the current trend in new car engine design toward double overhead camshafts is fully necessary simply to meet power, fuel economy, and emissions goals. "When you think of a double overhead cam V-8 with four valves per cylinder, that's a lot of hardware spinning around inside there: four camshafts, lots of timing chains or belts, 48 valves, and such. It all adds a lot of complexity and cost. I think it's all a little more complicated than it needs to be."

He also acknowledges that some of today's computerized engine management has put a damper on his business. "When you have computerized variable timing, in most cases, for both the intake and the exhaust valves, that does much of the work that a high-performance cam would do. Or for some of these engines, we'd need to make two or four cams and that adds a lot of cost for the customer. And engines that offer the ability to switch to a higher-performance camshaft profile while running, such as the Honda VTEC, makes it difficult to compete with the factory's development. So we don't see much play in the four-cam engine business."

Of course, the issues of fuel economy and emissions have presented certain challenges, but Ed says they are easily circumvented by multiple disclosures in catalogs and in product packaging that a particular cam is "For off-road use only" and from there, the company isn't responsible or liable for how the customer chooses to use the product.

Another interesting shift in the marketplace came with the demand and popularity for "RV cams." Intended primarily to perk up the low-end torque and performance of relatively low-compression truck and RV engines that came along in the 1970s, the RV cam became very popular among certain street muscle car enthusiasts and hot rodders who didn't drag race and were not as concerned with high-RPM power, but wanted low-end torque and grunt off the line. As the business shifted to meet this demand, so did Isky, with many of these "RV" grinds still listed in the current catalog.

HQ Today

To visit Isky Racing Cams headquarters today feels something like taking a walk through hot rodding and drag racing history. The rambling facility is part office, part production area (think of it as a combination between a machine and blacksmith's shop), a museum, and a junkyard. You can spend hours (and I have) simply absorbing the treasures in the lobby and counter area.

It's an amalgam of old photographs of Isky with a who's who of drag racing and dry lakes and Bonneville cars that run Isky cams. Most of the photos are frameless and casually taped up on the wall with little regard to placement or chronology. It is most charming in its casualness. There are dozens of trophies, plaques, awards, and testimonials honoring Ed or the company, or thanking them for their support in one way or another.

And as you might guess, there are camshafts sprinkled everywhere; the counter is a smorgasbord of cams, springs, timing gears, lifters, and assorted caminalia. You walk down the hallway at your own risk, because there's stuff everywhere.

I'm told that the rest of the car attached to this passenger-side door didn't survive an accident at the drags. Fortunately, the driver did and presented Ed with the remaining door. The Isky shop is a museum just waiting to happen. (Photo Courtesy Mel Stone)

In addition to walls full of great, faded photos of Isky customer cars, is this pristine enameled metal sign advertising Isky's Polydyne Profile Racing Cams. You don't have to look at too many Isky ads or promotional items to find the clever use of cartoon illustration. (Photo Courtesy Mel Stone)

The Isky Racing Cams lobby is overrun with the many accolades, trophies, awards, and recognition letters Ed and the company have received over the decades. (Photo Courtesy Mel Stone)

A computer terminal has likely replaced this wonderful old parts book stacker. Isky hasn't said they'll never print another catalog, but it's my guess that's the likely scenario, because it's much cheaper to produce the catalog in PDF form and save the cost of printing and mailing it, because distribution via the mysterious "interwebs" is largely free. Plus, online updates are faster and easier. But this approach, as old as the automotive parts house itself, is certainly charming if not as efficient. (Photo Courtesy Mel Stone)

The north hallway to the offices, design room, and the production shop is also filled with stuff as well as letters, photos, and news clippings casually taped to the wall. Note Ed's tinfoil ashtray at the lower left. Ed's stogie is omnipresent, but every once in a while, he lets one burn out and stores it here for future consumption. Remember: Never throw anything away; you don't know when you'll need it. (Photo Courtesy Mel Stone)

Until the Big Clean-Up of 2015, this is what the Isky Racing Cams lobby looked like right when you walked in the door. A bit of a mess, but a wonderful mess all the same. You'll recognize the big display cam on the wall from the photo on page 140 showing the same piece hung up at the first Dodger Stadium SEMA show.

Vic Edelbrock Jr. tells an amusing story about Ed and this particular office. (Note that there are two metal desks placed face to face.) Vic had a customer at his office one day, and the guy asked Vic to set him up with an Isky cam. Vic sent the customer to Gardena, with instructions to deal only with Ed.

The customer arrived and asked for Ed specifically, with instructions that Vic Edelbrock sent him. The counterman sent the hapless visitor to this office and told him to take a seat. The poor guy waited, and waited, and waited for Isky to arrive. After a while, he checked in again at the front desk, and it turns out that Isky was seated at the other desk the whole time. Through the dam of clutter, Ed didn't see or hear the customer walk in.

Goodness knows where this very 1950s-style nameplate may have been buried, but it was unearthed in the insurance inspector–mandated cleanup project of late 2015. Ed's offices are filled with such little statuettes, and all sorts of knickknacks that people bring or send him from all over the world.

The first office you pass on the left has a couple of desks that are piled 10 feet high with more of the same: cams, engine parts, engine blocks, heads, cigar boxes, papers, books, tools, and assorted machine shop miscellany.

The next office is the design office, somewhat similarly piled up with more of the same, although there is a path to get to the tables just in case someone may need to get to one in order to design or spec out a part. The bookshelves within contain books, parts manuals, old Isky catalogs, magazines; you name it.

The last large room down the north hallway is nearly impassable; the proverbial Fibber McGee's closet, at about 750 square feet. This, at one time, may have been a conference room.

A walk down the south hall leads to a large, "open" office area; Richard and Ron have desks there, as does office manager Ilene, marketing and online guy Nolan, and several other employees with a variety of jobs.

As Vic Edelbrock Jr. noted in the Foreword, it would be easy to label Ed as a packrat or a hoarder, which wouldn't be entirely untrue, but it's more than that; recall that Isky is a child of the stock market crash of 1929 and thus a child of the Depression and a family that didn't earn much more income than they needed just to survive. Ed is a 95-year-old example of "you don't throw anything away, because you'll never know when you'll need it."

The shop and production areas are more organized; leave the front office area and one of the first things you'll see is "Number-1," Ed's original cam-grinding machine, the very one on which the business was founded. Isky is very proud to show off this old machine, which "the old master" Ed Winfield taught him how to convert from a standard cylindrical grinder into a machine with a "rocking bar" head that can cut and grind the cam lobes. But it's not entirely just a showpiece or toehold of the company's beginnings. Ed says, "It still works, although of course it's fully manual with no computerized measuring or controls, but we still use it now and again for small jobs."

Take a walk along the production floor and you pass a variety of grinding and finishing machines, with busy machinist technicians and specialists working away, making one product or another, often accompanied by grinding noises and sparks flying. The area is reasonably well lit and generally clutter-free.

In the middle of the shop floor is an engine room, containing a wide variety of fully assembled engines, plus blocks, heads, and other engine assemblies. Lots of measuring and parts mocking takes place here. There are dynos for testing and other quality assurance measures.

Much of the south side of the main building is for inventory storage; completed cams and associated hardware, packaged and ready for shipment; newly finished pieces awaiting packaging; and racks of the raw bar stock that will someday be camshafts.

Leave the main building through the back door and you're in what resembles a junkyard full of old cars and machine shop bones from days gone by. Ancillary buildings hold a variety of other things,

The Isky production floor is a laid-back place, indicated by this big, happy smile and wave from longtime employee Thelma. Isky recalls that she's worked for the company for "around 30 years." (Photo Courtesy Mel Stone)

On the day of my visit, machinist specialist Thelma was straightening cams. In spite of the strong alloys used, and care given during production, cam cores become bent along the way, and obviously this creates all sorts of problems when it's installed in an engine. Ed's brother Ben says that a good tech can use instruments and gauges to determine where a cam is bent, and by how much. He adds, "The really good ones can eyeball it and tap it straight with a hammer and a round-nosed chisel" then spin the cam and use the gauges to verify that it's straight. Thelma appears to employ a bit of both methods. (Photo Courtesy Mel Stone)

Ron Iskenderian says that the surfacing of the cam lobes is different depending upon whether or not it is used with roller lifters and pushrods. The dark finish is for roller cam setups; the shiny polished finish is for conventional valvetrains. (Photo Courtesy Mel Stone)

A fully finished camshaft is indeed a bit of industrial artwork; note all of the machine operations that it takes to produce one. The end of the cam is drilled in a couple of places to properly index it to the timing gears. Of course, the lobes and bearing surfaces must be precision ground. The cam might need to be trued or straightened, and the lobes will ultimately be finished to ensure they don't wear out against the lifters.

Most Isky cams are stamped with the company imprint, model number, and other identification to protect against pirating, or someone trying to return or warranty claim a cam that was knocked off and not a true Iskenderian-produced product. Sounds strange, but it happens. (Photo Courtesy Mel Stone)

The engine room in the middle of the production floor houses a wide variety of fully assembled engines, as well as unfinished heads and blocks so parts can be test-fitted, tested, measured, or mocked-up as needed. (Photo Courtesy Mel Stone)

Isky machine specialist Charles is busy putting the surface finish on the non-geared ends of new cams. He is also cleaning up some cams that were returned as faulty or didn't pass their initial quality-assurance tests. He says that the problem is frequently minor and he can repair or clean up a fault on a customer cam so he or she may not need to replace it. (Photo Courtesy Mel Stone)

Cam surfacing detail is one part of the production floor that most resembles an old-school tool-and-die, or perhaps even a blacksmith, shop. It's working, grinding, finishing, polishing, and surfacing hard metal, with a tool, and often by hand. And who doesn't like watching a few sparks fly? (Photo Courtesy Mel Stone)

The little tag reads "Mr. Isky Cams. Don't Take." As with almost everything else, Isky has his own secret stash of cams; they could represent experimental things he is considering, old cams from hot rods and race cars gone by, some of his early production, whatever. If something sits on this cart, it belongs to The Boss and it's best left alone. Ed can look at a cam and by eye measurement alone tell you the lobe specs, and possibly what engine the piece fits. (Photo Courtesy Mel Stone)

Rack after rack of finished cams await packaging and shipping. If a specific piece isn't in stock, the production floor can turn one out in short order, but they know what sells in quantity, and in the largest numbers and most often, so a modest to medium inventory is always on hand. (Photo Courtesy Mel Stone)

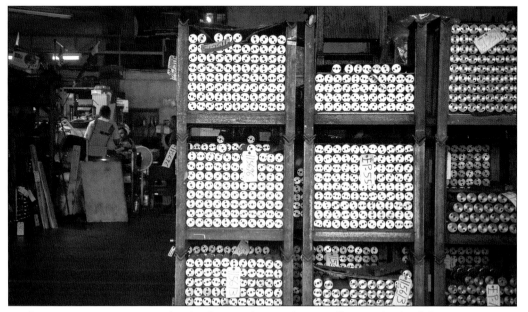

And even more cams in stock. This keeps the production flow and scheduling more even than would a "just in time" production scheme, which would make work schedules (and employee incomes) a lot more uneven. (Photo Courtesy Mel Stone)

Isky shows off an early homemade version of a valvetrain dynamometer. This machine only mounts the valvetrain of one cylinder to make the measurement, and then the power draw of this test is multiplied by the number of cylinders in the subject engine to determine the overall number. This folksy little machine served well until the company acquired its Spintron valvetrain dyno, which Ed credits as a major breakthrough in terms of valvetrain efficiency and durability testing. Isky bought one of the first machines, and now he claims that virtually every large engine builder in drag racing and NASCAR has them. (Photo Courtesy Mel Stone)

The engine room is filled with a variety of blocks and engines. This is a GM "corporate" small-block Chevy used in 4.8- and 5.3-liter engines. Isky Racing Cams doesn't offer engine-building services, but it is equipped to if the Iskenderian family ever decides to enter that business. (Photo Courtesy Mel Stone)

A recent photo shows Isky and an attractive young model showing off the 1962 Indy Nationals Class Winner's jacket. Ed is always happy to ham for the camera with a fan, customer, or racer, although we doubt this model was even born in 1962. (Photo Courtesy Ed Iskenderian)

The somewhat revolutionary Spintron machine earns its own special shed in back of the main shop so valvetrain dyno testing can continue without disturbing anything on the production floor. Note the aluminum NASCAR engine bolted to the back of the machine. The technician has been operating this machine for years and feels it's "priceless" in the development of efficient, low-resistance valvetrains; the engine has no carb, no exhaust, and no pistons inside because the engine doesn't actually run; it is turned by an instrumented electric motor that measures power draw inside the engine. (Photo Courtesy Mel Stone)

Isky leads the way to the Spintron shop and his personal outdoor treasure trove. Ed's cruiser beanie hat is omnipresent, and occasional bouts of poor circulation sometimes leave his hands a little cold, so he often wears gloves around the shop. (Photo Courtesy Mel Stone)

A mid-1970s Monza V-8 sunbathes in front of the '67 Cad. This Chevy model came with a very low compression, relatively low performance (350 ci when new), but the car doesn't weigh much so it felt fast at the time. It will make a great resto mod street car or bracket racer if Ed ever decides to let it out of the yard. Not likely anytime soon. (Photo Courtesy Mel Stone)

including more used or still-used machine equipment that should not sit out in the elements. One entire building is dedicated to the all-important Spintron machine, a critical element used in the development and durability testing of various valvetrain components.

Think of the Spintron as a sort of reverse dynamometer. Conventional dynos are designed to measure the horsepower and torque that an engine makes; this Spintron does the opposite: its primary purpose is to measure how much power a valvetrain uses. This is critical because reduced friction translates to increased power. During one particular visit, the Spintron was mounted with a General Motors NASCAR engine containing a camshaft and full valvetrain, but no pistons so the effects of compression don't affect the readings.

Beyond the buildings, extending back to the end of the property, is the wrecking yard; Ed calls this his treasure. Drill presses, lathes, milling machines, and a variety of equipment that's lived out its useful life. Plus mentor Ed Winfield's personal cam grinder. Air conditioning and cooling units, engine blocks, piles of cams, and a small plethora of old cars. Some are the used-up carcasses of Ed's own fleet; a couple of old Caddys here, a Lincoln there. A V-8 Chevy Monza, a mid-1950s Chevy pickup, a Saab Sonnett sports car.

I asked Ed, "Why the Saab?"

He said that he "bought it from a guy thinking it might make a good Bonneville car, being that it's small, light, and aerodynamic-looking."

Not an illogical set of conclusions, but they are as of yet unrealized, as the car sits, in non-running condition, bleaching in the sun, its date with a real dismantling junkyard in the future, as yet undetermined.

And Isky likes it this way, and he knows where *everything* is. Countless times I've asked him for a photo of

This looks like a pile of scrap metal junk to me, but not to Ed Iskenderian. Isky knows what most of this equipment is, what it does, if it works, and where it came from, although I'd guess that a few of Gardena's older supermarkets are wondering what happened to their shopping carts. (Photo Courtesy Mel Stone)

This hulking 1950s Chevy pickup is "all there," as they say, but needs plenty of work to be brought back to health and beauty. There's no rust deeper than the surface, and all the glass is unbroken, so it would look great refinished in red, white, and blue as an Isky shop truck tribute. (Photo Courtesy Mel Stone)

One of Ed's many dead Caddys. This monster '67 could be saved, but it would be a long and expensive road back. But as a California sunbaked rust-free parts car? Now you're talking. (Photo Courtesy Mel Stone)

I'm only guessing, but I'd say that this mid-1970s Chevy pickup has rolled its last mile under its own power. (Photo Courtesy Mel Stone)

It just wouldn't be Isky's back lot without a flathead V-8 block sitting around. The white marker notes on the bellhousing is evidence that this block has already been bored 100 thousandths over. Given that a flathead usually runs out of good structural cylinder meat at around 60 thousandths, this block is likely lawn sculpture or scrap metal by now. (Photo Courtesy Mel Stone)

something, and he'd walk into one of the packed-to-the-gills offices and pull it out of a pile or file cabinet. He can walk through the backyard and name off every cast-off piece of machinery that sits there. Some he bought in the early days of his business, other things only because they attracted him or were an especially good deal.

And so everything sits. Or sat, until one day in the fall of 2015, when his fire insurance policy was up for renewal. For some reason, his carrier sent an inspector to see the property, and after a tour of the office areas, some with hallways too narrowed to safely navigate, the insurance company threatened not to renew his policy. So Ed was forced to "clean up his room."

He and a team of employees started at the lobby and then attacked the back offices. They divided things into three piles: items that would stay inside, items that would be relocated to a storage container outside the main buildings, and

The first time I peeked in the door of this office, I wasn't sure if it had carpeting or not. After the Great Insurance Clean-Up of 2015, I saw the floor for the first time and discovered very old, but still intact, industrial office carpeting. Wow! (Photo Courtesy Mel Stone)

Judging by the piles on this drafting table, it's likely that no new design work has taken place in quite some time, or will anytime soon. No fear, that's what computer-aided design is for, something Isky Racing Cams adopted a long time ago. (Photo Courtesy Mel Stone)

Everybody needs a room-size junk drawer. (Photo Courtesy Mel Stone)

trash. For Isky this was a terribly stressful process, as I often heard him admonishing his employees not to throw anything out without checking with him first. Suddenly, the rooms and hallways became larger, and floor, table, and desk space magically appeared.

I complimented Ed on the transformation, and he said that yes, "It's nice to have more room, but I'm afraid I won't be able to find stuff when I want it." It's still cluttered in a well-used, charming way, but at least there are places to sit here and there. And Isky Racing Cams has fire insurance.

Fortunately, the continued popularity of timeless overhead valve engines, such as the small- and big-block Chevrolet V-8s, the small-block Ford, and the continued popularity of drag racing and Bonneville top-speed racing, keep Isky (the man and the company) plenty busy. Plus the many Chrysler wedge and Hemi V-8s. The growth of nostalgic "traditional" hot rodding has also brought about increased demand for Isky's flathead Ford V-8 grinds. Yes, you can still buy a classic Isky 404 cam.

To that point, I quote the renowned traditional hot rod builder Vern Tardel, who said in his excellent book *How to Build a Traditional Ford Hot Rod*, co-authored with Mike Bishop, "Isky also continues to grind some of the best-ever flat-engine cams. For street applications, we like both the 3/4 race Max 1 and the 400-JR. The milder Max1 scarcely lopes at idle, and

You might name this old machine "Grandpa Grinder" because it originally belonged to Isky's legendary mentor, Ed Winfield. Much like Isky's first cam-grinding machine, this one began life as a cylindrical grinder and was converted by its owner/operator with a self-fabricated "rocking bar" attachment so it could draw cam lobe profiles from a "master" pattern, and then grind them on to the bar stock that ultimately became a camshaft. Isky owns Winfield's old machine and keeps it as a tribute to the man he considers "The Old Master."

Ed sits in his fabulous hot rod, looking at an article in Hot Rod *magazine in which this very car was featured inside and on the cover. The bespeckled young man wearing the Isky T-shirt and holding the magazine is the late A. B. Schuman, one of the very best to ever call himself an automotive scribe. Shuman also edited Petersen's* Car Craft *magazine and enjoyed a distinguished 20-year career in automotive public and media relations with Mercedes-Benz. (Photo Courtesy TEN: The Enthusiast Network Archive)*

This wonderful wood carving shows what is likely a cam-grinding machine, produced by the Axelson Manufacturing Company, Los Angeles, California. It bears one of Ed's catch phrases: "There is no economical substitute for quality." The work is beautifully turned and well preserved, and signed in the lower left corner, "George Ernst, 1943." Cool in anyone's book or in anyone's shop. (Photo Courtesy Mel Stone)

Isky loves to fish, and seldom missed Petersen Publishing's annual fishing trip. This is vintage Ed, on a fishing boat, chomping on a stogie, and wearing a bleached and faded Iskenderian Racing Cams T-shirt. To his left is Ray Brock, editor of Hot Rod *at the time. (Photo Courtesy TEN: The Enthusiast Network Archive)*

With "nostalgia" drag racing more popular than ever, and the hot rod community favoring "traditional" hot rods, Isky Racing Cams ads make the most of its biggest asset, the Camfather himself. The company still produces cam and equipment for engine families that many other companies have forgotten about or left behind. Isky can still grind up nearly any profile his company has ever produced. (Photo Courtesy Ed Iskenderian)

In this ad, the company again banks on its heritage as having produced its products since the middle of the previous century. This is a rare generic ad; Ed normally likes to mention specific products in his marketing and/or feature tech tips or cars other than his own. But it works. (Photo Courtesy Ed Iskenderian)

ED ISKENDERIAN RACING CAMS

THE WORLD'S LARGEST FACILITY FOR DESIGN, TEST AND PRODUCTION OF

RACING CAMS

16020 So. Broadway, Gardena, Calif. 90248
Tel (213) 770-0930

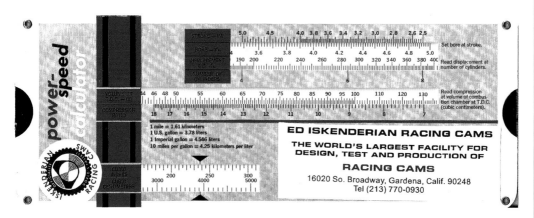

One of Isky's clever marketing tools are these little performance "computers," which are handy slide rules and wheel calculators that recommend all sorts of things such as compression and the ideal rear end ratio. Edelbrock's dyno guys (Kurt Hooker and Robert Jung) testify that these are much more than toys, and often provide very good starting points in setting up a car. They each have one in their toolbox to this day. (Photo Courtesy Ed Iskenderian)

This is textbook Isky: leaving his favorite Los Angeles burger joint, just a little disheveled, four pounds of stuff in his shirt pocket, and the last half of his pre-lunch cigar ready to refire and puff during the afternoon. Hmm . . . and about that haircut. Buzzed on the sides and furry up top; going for the mohawk look there, Ed? (Photo Courtesy Ed Iskenderian)

it's a good fuel mileage grind in spite of a noticeable performance improvement. But for our money, the 400-JR, with its great snap and rumpety idle is the cam to have. The fuel economy penalty of a few miles per gallon is easily offset by much stronger acceleration than the Max 1. And, of course, there's that wonderful sound!"

Last Words

Ed Iskenderian reminds us:

- Don't be ashamed of your accomplishments. If you did something great, if you went faster, or won the race, don't hesitate to let people know.
- Complacency can be lethal. I believe one of the reasons we were so successful early on is that we kept driving toward something new and, we hoped, better. For a while, there weren't that many players in the cam-grinding game, and some of the guys were selling every part they could produce and deliver. So they became a little lazy. We may have been a lot of things, but we were never lazy about serving the customer; and we didn't wait around for someone to do something better than us.
- Cam grinding is some part science, some part math, some part luck, and a big part educated guesswork.
- Don't be afraid to try something unusual; it might not work, but it might also lead you to something great.
- Don't compromise quality to save cost.
- Honest competition is generally healthy for everyone involved, but keep it friendly.
- Work hard, but make sure to take some time off to go fishing.
- Sometimes you win, and sometimes you blow up.
- Hot rodding and racing have been awfully good to me. Sometimes it was just a matter of going out there and trying something. Eventually, you might stumble onto something that works.

Just in case you are under the impression that drag racing is only a young person's game, check out 95-year-old Ed Iskenderian working the Nostalgia Drags starting line at Eagle Field near Firebaugh, California, on Saturday, May 21, 2016. He was flag starting 90-year-old Elmer "Unsprung" Snyder who always makes the first pass at Eagle Field driving his flathead dragster from the 1950s.

In the days before the invention of the popular "Christmas Tree" staging and starting light system, drag races were started by the waving of a flag, or sometimes the waving of a scarf by an attractive young woman (or the turning on and off of a flashlight if the action took place at night). Invariably the flag wavers developed their own flamboyant style of jumping in the air as they waved the flag starting the race. It's nice to see that even though he's just a few years shy of 100, Isky's still got the jump thing down. (Photos Courtesy Dave Kommel)

Chapter 7

PROMOTE, PROMOTE, PROMOTE!

Ed felt he had to be careful in his earliest advertisements because, of course, in the beginning, he hadn't done anything or won anything. But when his customers began winning big races, Ed wasn't shy about touting those accomplishments in his ads and promotional materials. (Photo Courtesy Ed Iskenderian)

Ed Iskenderian never had any formal education in the fields of marketing, advertising, or public relations. However, these are aspects of his business for which he has long displayed a natural, instinctive knack, and something he enjoyed immensely. His business was just learning to walk when *Hot Rod* magazine was born in the late 1940s, and he immediately knew he had to advertise in its pages. He remembers his first ads (see Chapter 3), which were just a column wide and a few inches long, costing $20 and $30 per issue.

Moreover, Isky was pleasantly surprised when he received a response. "I was still a kid trying to bluff my way into the camshaft business," he recalls now, "and I guess some people might have figured that since I was out in California where all the hot rod action was, I really knew what I was doing."

Isky liberally credits talented ad and creative teams that developed his ever-evolving promotional materials and messaging. His ads and flyers took on a variety of tones, from the more serious "Race with the Winners" to the lighthearted, often-whimsical cartoon-style ads. He always felt it was smart to point out his accomplishments and highlight the big wins of drivers and teams that he supported. "If you've done something really good, why be shy about it?"

Isky has never condoned out-and-out lying or making up records that don't exist, but he absolutely believes in the power of advertising. When Don Garlits renamed his car the "Iskenderian Camshaft Special" and was really winning big, Ed knew this was ad-worthy and featured the fast Floridian as a primary subject of some of his ad layouts. He later learned that some of the drivers and cars highlighted in his ads were, on occasion, being paid "appearance money" to compete at certain events. He was pleased that "his guys" were making a little extra money on the deal and spreading the word further about his products.

Although some of his advertisements featured cartoons and other lighthearted bits of humor, Ed always felt that other

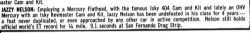

This full-page ad from 1956 was a big step up for Iskenderian Racing Cams; it gave the company a lot more space to share news about its products, and to offer op-ed and provide technical information. Power adders for Ford's still relatively new Y-block V-8 (found in a variety of Fords and Mercurys, including the hot new Thunderbird) dominate this layout. Note the props and plug for "Jazzy" Jim Nelson's Isky-cammed, flathead-powered Fiat Topolino drag racer, a longtime Isky favorite. (Photo Courtesy Ed Iskenderian)

printed materials, particularly his catalogs, needed to be top-quality presentations.

Each year's catalog featured a uniquely designed cover, often with special artwork just for that issue, and the photos, graphs, and layouts inside were first-rate, high-quality, magazine-style pages. In addition to just listing all of the products, costs, and applications, those spreads always included a considerable amount of "how-to," installation, and technical information, as well as photos and information about his large, high-tech research, development, and production facilities.

Advertising always proved to be particularly beneficial for Ed's company,

and as time went by, he invested more and more into his ad programs, developing ever-larger ad spreads, and running them in more and more publications. By the late 1950s, he had developed expensive, expansive full-page ads, and was running full-page ads in *Hot Rod* "just like a real grown-up car company," he recalls. This type of marketing is expensive, especially for a relatively small company; each issue cost several thousand dollars a month. Ed recalls one period when he ran single full-page ads in 40 consecutive issues of *Hot Rod*, at a total cost of more than $100,000 in late-1950s dollars.

Iskenderian Cams' catalogs are always richly illustrated and beautifully produced. Some covers are composed of photos and type, others have colorful illustrations or paintings. This is from 1968; the cover price of just a buck! (Photo Courtesy Ed Iskenderian)

Ed is justifiably proud of his facilities, staff, equipment, quality development, and testing operations. This page from the 1968 catalog shows his Gardena location, several production and testing areas within the shop, and the names and faces of several key employees. (Photo Courtesy Ed Iskenderian)

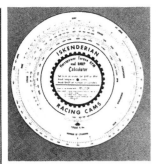

ISKY B.M.E.P. CALCULATOR

Here is a tuning aid designed for the dyno technician, automotive engineer and master mechanic. By setting the indicator to show the rpm at which your engine achieved its horsepower, the calculator converts this into torque and also Break Mean Effective Pressure. **$2.50**

ISKY SPEED AND RATIO COMPUTER

The average speed computer is a must for all race fans. Quickly figures average speed by dialing in track distance and elapsed time. The reverse side accurately figures compression ratios and engine displacement. **$1.50**

ISKY IRON-ON TRANSFERS

Make your own Isky T-shirts and sweatshirts in just a few minutes. Big iron-on transfer is beautifully printed in red and black just like the original Isky T-shirt. Using a moderately hot iron, the design is permanently transferred to the cloth and is colorfast and washable. Two for . **$ .25**
Iron-on Special: 12 for **$1.00**

ISKY T-SHIRT

Big "I" emblem on front in orange and black and racing bars on back in red and black. Made in U.S.A. of 100% cotton. Printing is colorfast and washable. Available in the following sizes: midget, small, medium, large, extra large. . . . . .net **$1.50** each
Car clubs and other groups can have their own custom design T-shirts with club name printed on front and Isky emblem on back. Write to the Technical Aid Department for details and club discount prices.

ISKY NYLON RACER'S JACKET

This popular Isky jacket is made of high quality material with a warm fleece lining. It's lightweight for comfort, yet will keep you warm on those chilly days and nights. Has two colorful patches on front and back and is available in   green or blue. available in small, medium, large or extra large...net **$10.00**

109

This catalog page shows some of the Isky merchandise available, including the "ratio computers," handsome racing jackets (at just $10), and the Isky Racing Cams T-shirts, the design of which evolved a lot through the years. Among the best known is the "Big I" design, so named for the obvious reason. (Photo Courtesy Ed Iskenderian)

ISKENDERIAN UNIVERSALLY RECOGNIZED
...AS A Major Contributor to Automotive Engineering and Advancement

For the past decade and a half Iskenderian has consistently maintained a program of progressive engineering and development in the racing camshaft field. This dedicated adherence has not gone unnoticed, even in the upper echelons of the automotive industry. Iskenderian has achieved noticeable success in a highly critical area of engine modification — and this success has been duly recognized.

Firestone Tire Company

Firestone maintains a full time experimental division under the supervision of engineer, Ray Nichols, to test their products. Since it is the purpose of this program to conduct tests at the highest speeds and maximum acceleration they equip their cars with finest in the way of speed equipment. Their experimental division has called upon Iskenderian to supply racing cams for these tests.

DETROIT, MICHIGAN

Up till recently the nation's largest automobile manufacturers subsidized and sponsored racing teams to publicize the power potential of their products. Tests under the most severe conditions were conducted to evaluate dependability and performance. These manufacturers requisitioned their racing cams almost 100% from the firm of Ed Iskenderian, although products from other grinders were tested for preliminary comparison.

EUROPEAN and FOREIGN COUNTRIES

Numerous chief librarians and heads of automotive technical departments throughout Europe have sent in direct requests for further data and literature on racing camshafts. In fact Ed Iskenderian's own book 'Valve Timing for Maximum Output' may be found on the shelves of some of the most well-known automotive technical libraries in Europe today, as well as those in the United States and other countries.

DESMODROMIC
VALVE GEAR ENGINEERING

An exclusive specialized service for Racing Car Manufacturers to develop Sport Car Conversions. Successfully used by several European Car Manufacturers. Relieves factory engineers of the highly complicated and endless· trigometric calculations in developing Desmodromic Valve Gear.

WRITE . . . OR WIRE FOR SPECIFIC INFORMATION

ENGLAND

Staid and proud Englishmen yielded a reluctant point in camshaft engineering when they solicited information from the firm of Ed Iskenderian. Isky's unprecedented success in camshafts developed for British cars was responsible for some of the major car manufacturers importing these cams for use in their own racing and experimental cars.

Jaguar factory racing teams, represented in the U.S.A. by Briggs Cunningham and Momo Corp., employ Iskenderian cams exclusively in the 'D' Jaguars. For engine dyno test reports released by factory, see below.

TYPICAL PERFORMANCE TESTS

MGA (Production Class Sports Car Racer)
Chassis Dynamometer Tests

STOCK CAM: Developed peak horsepower of **42 HP** at rear wheels at **5000 rpm.** Power fell off thereafter.

ISKY T3 CAM and ENGINEERED KIT: Developed peak horsepower of **61 HP** at rear wheels at **6000 rpm.** Power fell off after 6000 rpm. Max. revs without valve float 7000 rpm.

MODIFIED JAGUAR (FACTORY ENGINE DYNAMOMETER TESTS)
Cam used: Isky XM2
Maximum Torque: 282 Ft. Lbs. at 4500 rpm. **Bore:** 87.3mm **Stroke:** 106mm
Displacement: 3801 cc. (approx.) **Carburetion:** 3 Weber 45mm, DCO3
Engine: D Type (modified) **Compression ratio:** 10 to 1 **Distributor:** Lucas
Fuel: 100 Octane pump gas

BRAKE HORSEPOWER:

1000 rpm — 38.2 hp	3000 rpm — 140.0 hp	5000 rpm — 265.0 hp
1500 rpm — 63.5 hp	3500 rpm — 170.2 hp	5500 rpm — 276.5 hp
2000 rpm — 82.3 hp	4000 rpm — 208.2 hp	5750 rpm — 283.0 hp
2500 rpm — 112.7 hp	4500 rpm — 243.0 hp	6000 rpm — 284.0 hp

REMARKS: Idling slightly faster than stock but smooth.

74

"ISKENDERIAN ENGINEERING MAKES THE DIFFERENCE"

This ad is somewhat institutional in nature, underpinning Isky's relationship with big OEM companies such as Firestone. It also does some noodling around with exotic "desmodromic" valvetrains, which do away with conventional valvesprings, and open and close the valves via gears. Plus, it mentions Isky's products for English and European manufacturers. (Photo Courtesy Ed Iskenderian)

This 1973 catalog has obviously lived a hard life, but shows some typical 1970s-style product photography, in this case it's Isky's main product, camshafts, of course. (Photo Courtesy Ed Iskenderian)

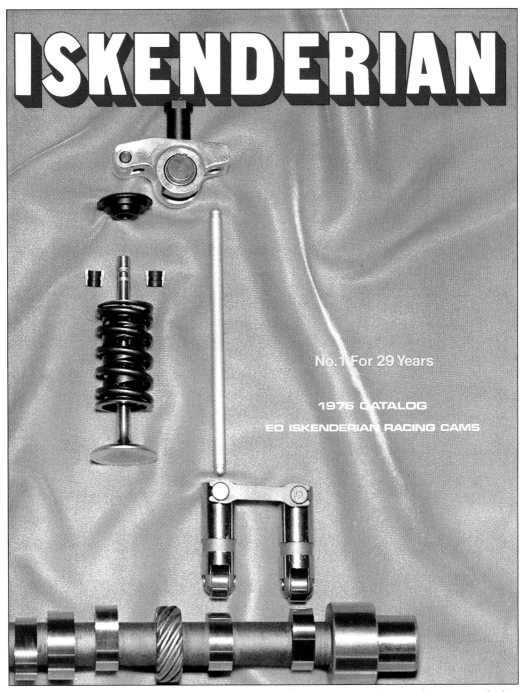

This 1976 catalog cover shows the main points of a modern "rocker" valvetrain, including the camshaft, roller lifters, adjustable pushrods, the valvespring, and roller rocker arms at the top. (Photo Courtesy Ed Iskenderian)

ISKY

THE NAME THAT IS SYNONYMOUS WITH HOT RODDING

THE ISKY CAR OF THE MONTH

This month's winner is **Tom McMurphy** of **Chico, Calif.** He sent us a photo of his sharp street/strip car and this letter: "In 1964, I bought an **Iskenderian E-4 cam** and slipped it into a 283 Chevy block. The 283 found its way into my 1955 Chevy, and my tach read 1500 decimals higher than before the Isky was installed. The cam has been well worth the cost, it now has over 45,000 miles, and it shows only normal wear. The little engine still pulls over 6500 rpm's with ease. The last time I went dragging was about a year ago, the Isky equipped Chevy brought home the gold. This cam has been through almost every type of driving from screaming at the drags, to plowing through snow drifts, to loping down the main drag to impress the troops; it has been more than satisfactory in every situation."

AN ISKY CAM FOR $55!

Iskenderian offers a full range of cams for the 283-327-350 Chevrolet engines. From the street driveable 280° hydraulic and RPM-300 flat tappet (priced at only $55), to the all-out competition 555 Invincible hardface and roller cams. These Isky grinds were developed after extensive testing on the Iskenderian dynamometer. **For complete information. Send 10c for eight page Chevrolet engine cam spec sheet.**

NEW ISKY CATALOG

The largest catalog of high performance automotive equipment, featuring the world's largest stock of racing cams and related speed equipment. Info on most engines incl. imports, tuning tips, etc. 120 pages. Send $2.00 and get a $1.50 Isky Ratio Computer.

ED ISKENDERIAN

RACING CAMS

16020 SOUTH BROADWAY ■ GARDENA, CALIF. 90247

Dept. RC

Innovative, if somewhat different from the company's norm, this long, single-column ad featured a car of the month, a '55 Chevrolet, and advertised a special cam deal, for $55. A brief pitch at the bottom announced the availability of a new catalog. Simple, cool, and to the point. (Photo Courtesy Ed Iskenderian)

This is another example of the high-quality production values of Isky's promotional materials. This special brochure highlights the company's dynamometer-proven results showing several pages of power graphs obtained from Isky-cammed engines. The cover of this multipage color brochure is a beautiful painting of an SOHC 427 Ford engine running on the dyno (of course). This handsome brochure also describes the equipment and processes used to test for these results. The proof is in the pudding; the numbers don't lie. (Photo Courtesy Ed Iskenderian)

WHAT DYNO TESTING MEANS TO YOU

The Iskenderian dynamometer testing facility was specifically set up to accurately test and prove every one of our new cam designs before any are manufactured or sold. And, because it is the only specialized facility of its kind in the cam manufacturing industry, you can be assured when purchasing an Isky cam that you are getting a product of proven highest quality and performance.

Iskenderian engineers maintain a constant schedule of testing and evaluating the newest and most popular engines. Each test is recorded and conducted under controlled atmospheric conditions so that highly accurate horsepower readings may be gained from any given engine configuration. Dyno testing procedures, which may take up to three months to perfect one cam design, are tailored to your exact requirements. Cam design changes, engine modifications and additions of high performance speed equipment are made so that you can be sure of getting the most 'cam power' for your car, whether it be for street, street and strip or all-out competition.

The exact results of these tests have been reproduced on special dyno graphs (included in this book) with all pertinent engine information and are included free with each cam. Iskenderian technicians conduct the dyno tests with varying combinations of ignition settings, spark plugs, carburetion and jet sizes with the end result a valuable book of Tuning Tips so that you can get all the horsepower for which the cam is rated. Our dyno is also a tough test of major brands of speed equipment and the hot engine builder gets valuable information on intake manifolds, carburetors, headers, ignitions, pistons, rings, rods, bearings and much more.

Another equally important phase of our development program is the 'compatibility' testing of Isky valve train components such as tappets (lifters), push rods, rocker arms, valve springs, retainers and keepers. Our engineers refer to our second dynamometer as the "Wear Out Dyno" because of the extreme punishment to which we subject all valve train components. Spring pressures up to 600 pounds (valve open) have been continuously conducted to determine the exact combination and types of hardening that will result in long, dependable high performance.

During the past eight years of dynamometer cam improvement many significant breakthroughs have been made by Iskenderian technicians. Parkerizing (an acid bath which etches the cam and at the same time coats it with a non-metallic lubricant) and Dry-Lube (a lubricant that is baked onto the cam) were both discovered to greatly increase cam life. Another Isky development is Cam Lube which eliminates scuffing and wear during the first few critical minutes of engine running, and it will continue to protect your prized engine by adding it at regular oil change intervals. By using these dyno-proven combinations, Iskenderian Racing Cams is the first and only cam manufacturer to offer a four-year cam warranty.

We at Iskenderian sincerely believe that the dyno is a necessary precision tool in the perfection of a camshaft.

Ed believes in transparency with his customers, giving them results and "no bull." This page explains why the customer should care about, and demand, dyno-proven results. (Photo Courtesy Ed Iskenderian)

OUR TESTING PROGRAM

To properly evaluate an engine's potential and to effectively design racing cams and valve train components, every new engine that is introduced by automobile manufacturers is purchased and subjected to a planned program of dyno testing.

To begin with, Iskenderian engineers use a modern high speed electronic computer to work out all new cam formulas. It was with the use of such a computer that the Polydyne formula (used by Iskenderian) was developed and has since proven to be a revolutionary advancement in cam engineering. Next, a model cam is made. This step is more an art of the trade than a science and relates directly to the experience of the cam manufacturer. Here, Iskenderian has over 20 years of high performance cam creational experience. From the model cam a precision master is ground and from this a single experimental lobe is made for testing on the Electronic Stroboscopic Testing Machine. With this machine, Iskenderian technicians can visually observe the action of the cam and what the valve is doing at any given rpm over a full engine range. Stroboscopic viewing is a means of synchronizing the intermittent flashing of a beam of light with the speed of the parts under observation. When this occurs, the parts in motion present a visual illusion of being motionless.

With the actions of the complete valve train revealed, our technicians then make all necessary corrections and a full test cam is produced. It is then installed in an engine and degreed for correct valve opening and closing (phasing). Valve-to-piston clearance is carefully checked and we also check to make sure there is no valve spring coil bind. If everything is according to calculations, the engine is then 'fired' and a full range of dyno tests are run under controlled laboratory conditions. Tests are run up to 7500 rpm at 500 rpm increments. Special evaluations are made at 100 rpm increments and all tests are made with various spark and valve lash settings to find the maximum horsepower. These readings are compared against what we call a ''base line'' cam which is our best grind prior to the development of a new camshaft. Further testing includes carburetion, ignition, plugs, headers and high performance modifications according to cam grind.

From start to finish, our development program sometimes takes as long as three months and consumes over 500 man-hours, including the actual production of 25 or more experimental cams to achieve the ONE which is qualified to wear the Isky Seal.

Before each dyno run, Iskenderian technicians check every component, make planned program changes and accurately set tolerances so the slightest hp change can be precisely noted.

The control factor in comparing cams and speed equipment is our highly sensitive and specialized gauges. Before each run the barometer, air wet, air dry and vapor pressure is accurately noted.

Along with dyno proving our cams, all shapes and sizes of headers are tested as well as major brands of speed equipment. This becomes a valuable service to our customers as Iskenderian can recommend the best equipment to give you the most horsepower.

Here is more information from the same brochure about Isky's testing procedures and equipment; note the use of computer-controlled equipment in the middle photo, something highly innovative and advanced when computers were thought to be only really necessary for defense contractors and the space administration. (Photo Courtesy Ed Iskenderian)

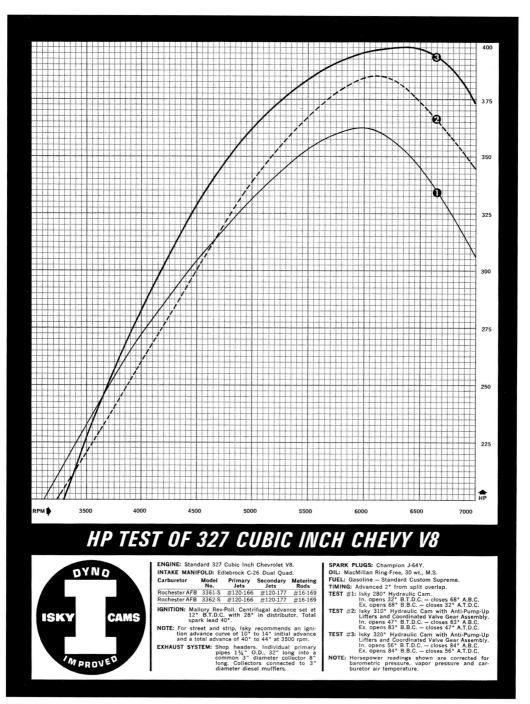

HP TEST OF 327 CUBIC INCH CHEVY V8

ENGINE: Standard 327 Cubic Inch Chevrolet V8.
INTAKE MANIFOLD: Edlebrock C-26 Dual Quad.

Carburetor	Model No.	Primary Jets	Secondary Jets	Metering Rods
Rochester AFB	3361-S	#120-166	#120-177	#16-169
Rochester AFB	3362-S	#120-166	#120-177	#16-169

IGNITION: Mallory Rev-Poll. Centrifugal advance set at 12° B.T.D.C. with 28° in distributor. Total spark lead 40°.

NOTE: For street and strip, Isky recommends an ignition advance curve of 10° to 14° initial advance and a total advance of 40° to 44° at 3500 rpm.

EXHAUST SYSTEM: Shop headers. Individual primary pipes 1¾" O.D., 32" long into a common 3" diameter collector 8" long. Collectors connected to 3" diameter diesel mufflers.

SPARK PLUGS: Champion J-64Y.
OIL: MacMillan Ring-Free, 30 wt., M.S.
FUEL: Gasoline — Standard Custom Supreme.
TIMING: Advanced 2° from split overlap.
TEST #1: Isky 280° Hydraulic Cam.
    In. opens 32° B.T.D.C. — closes 68° A.B.C.
    Ex. opens 68° B.B.C. — closes 32° A.T.D.C.
TEST #2: Isky 310° Hydraulic Cam with Anti-Pump-Up Lifters and Coordinated Valve Gear Assembly.
    In. opens 47° B.T.D.C. — closes 83° A.B.C.
    Ex. opens 83° B.B.C. — closes 47° A.T.D.C.
TEST #3: Isky 320° Hydraulic Cam with Anti-Pump-Up Lifters and Coordinated Valve Gear Assembly.
    In. opens 56° B.T.D.C. — closes 84° A.B.C.
    Ex. opens 84° B.B.C. — closes 56° A.T.D.C.
NOTE: Horsepower readings shown are corrected for barometric pressure, vapor pressure and carburetor air temperature.

Dyno curve results for the ever-popular 327 Chevy small-block V-8. (Photo Courtesy Ed Iskenderian)

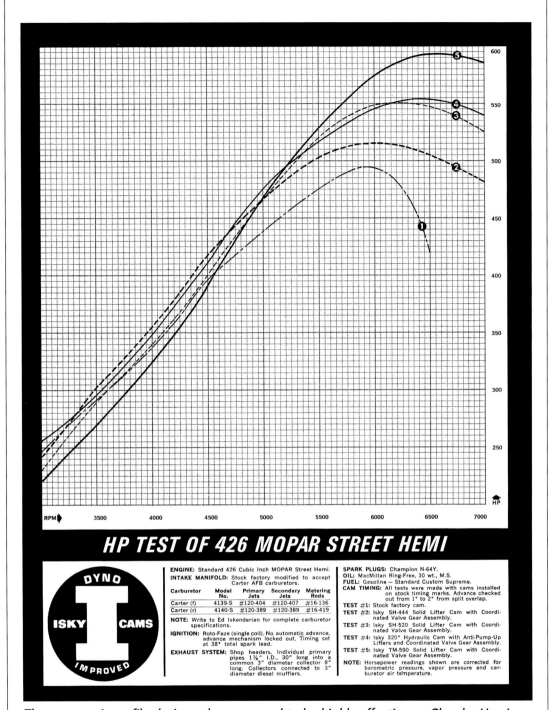

HP TEST OF 426 MOPAR STREET HEMI

ENGINE: Standard 426 Cubic Inch MOPAR Street Hemi.

INTAKE MANIFOLD: Stock factory modified to accept Carter AFB carburetors.

Carburetor	Model No.	Primary Jets	Secondary Jets	Metering Rods
Carter (f)	4139-S	#120-404	#120-407	#16-136
Carter (r)	4140-S	#120-389	#120-389	#16-419

NOTE: Write to Ed Iskenderian for complete carburetor specifications.

IGNITION: Roto-Faze (single coil). No automatic advance, advance mechanism locked out. Timing set at 38° total spark lead.

EXHAUST SYSTEM: Shop headers. Individual primary pipes 1⅞" I.D., 30" long into a common 3" diameter collector 8" long. Collectors connected to 3" diameter diesel mufflers.

SPARK PLUGS: Champion N-64Y.

OIL: MacMillan Ring-Free, 30 wt., M.S.

FUEL: Gasoline — Standard Custom Supreme.

CAM TIMING: All tests were made with cams installed on stock timing marks. Advance checked out from 1" to 2" from split overlap.

TEST #1: Stock factory cam.

TEST #2: Isky SH-444 Solid Lifter Cam with Coordinated Valve Gear Assembly.

TEST #3: Isky SH-520 Solid Lifter Cam with Coordinated Valve Gear Assembly.

TEST #4: Isky 320° Hydraulic Cam with Anti-Pump-Up Lifters and Coordinated Valve Gear Assembly.

TEST #5: Isky TM-590 Solid Lifter Cam with Coordinated Valve Gear Assembly.

NOTE: Horsepower readings shown are corrected for barometric pressure, vapor pressure and carburetor air temperature.

The company's profile designs always proved to be highly effective on Chrysler Hemi engines: both the early, first-generation street Hemis and the later 426-ci "Elephant" Street Hemi V-8s. (Photo Courtesy Ed Iskenderian)

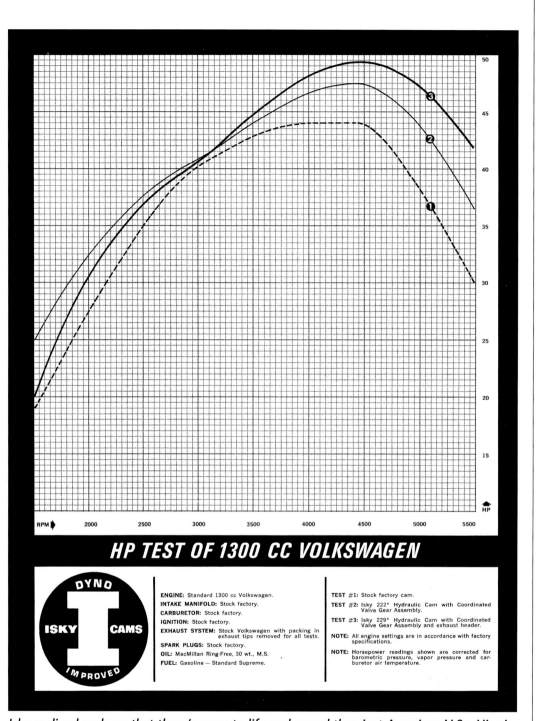

HP TEST OF 1300 CC VOLKSWAGEN

ENGINE: Standard 1300 cc Volkswagen.
INTAKE MANIFOLD: Stock factory.
CARBURETOR: Stock factory.
IGNITION: Stock factory.
EXHAUST SYSTEM: Stock Volkswagen with packing in exhaust tips removed for all tests.
SPARK PLUGS: Stock factory.
OIL: MacMillan Ring-Free, 30 wt., M.S.
FUEL: Gasoline — Standard Supreme.

TEST #1: Stock factory cam.
TEST #2: Isky 222° Hydraulic Cam with Coordinated Valve Gear Assembly.
TEST #3: Isky 229° Hydraulic Cam with Coordinated Valve Gear Assembly and exhaust header.
NOTE: All engine settings are in accordance with factory specifications.
NOTE: Horsepower readings shown are corrected for barometric pressure, vapor pressure and carburetor air temperature.

Isky realized early on that there's more to life and speed than just American V-8s. His air-cooled VW cams yielded impressive performance gains. (Photo Courtesy Ed Iskenderian)

ABOUT THE DYNO

The focal point of Iskenderian Racing Cams custom built dynamometer facility is our Taylor Hi-Eff (high efficiency) Dyno. It's of the water brake type and is run by a special drive shaft direct from the engine's flywheel. By taking full advantage of our over eight years of dyno testing, Isky engineers have modified the Taylor and its related precision equipment to the exact needs of our exclusive testing program.

The Taylor dyno can handle engines up to 1,200 horsepower and over 8,000 rpm. However, even now, this capacity is being increased to be ready for the higher demands of tomorrow's all-out competition engines.

To help us maintain the high degree of precision in our testing program, a variety of highly sensitive and specialized gauges monitor every vital engine function. These precision gauges are the control factor for proving the horsepower and dependability you expect from the world's leading cam manufacturer... ISKY.

Right. Our third and newest dyno is a Stuska which is used to dyno prove all equipment for small displacement and foreign car engines. It can safely handle engines up to 350 hp and 9,000 rpm. The Stuska features its own console with torque scale, tachometer, throttle and starter.

Below. The control panel gauges from left to right are the torque scale, air inlet temperature, rpm accumulator, tach, running time accumulator, vacuum-boost gauge, oil temperature, oil pressure, fuel pressure pump, fuel pressure, foot pounds scale, throttle, starter and ignition switch.

The Taylor Hi-Efficiency Dynamometer and its related precision equipment have been highly refined over the past eight years to the exact needs of our exclusive testing program. The universal mounts, controls and gauges can handle any automotive engine and an engine can be set-up, ready-to-run in a few hours. Our dyno can safely handle engines up to 1,200 horsepower and over 8,000 rpm. We have even tested such related items as oil filters, oil pans and ignition wire with these helpful tips being found in our Top Tuners Manual.

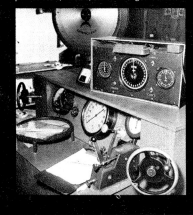

N/D 3-68 PRINTED IN U.S.A.

The company had several dynos able to accommodate engines from the smallest 4-cylinder to the largest, strongest drag racing powerplants. (Photo Courtesy Ed Iskenderian)

ISKENDERIAN

"TOP TUNER'S TIPS" BY ED ISKENDERIAN...AS THEY APPEARED

ISKY CAMS

IN HOT ROD AND OTHER RODDING MAGAZINES

Top Tuner's Tips

Every engine needs its T.D.C.! It's easy to spot today's novice engine builder because he invariably neglects to calibrate his engine for T.D.C. (Top Dead Center of the No. 1 piston). This T.D.C. mark is the all important starting point from which all ignition and valve timing reference is based. Even stock engines are factory equipped with a T.D.C. mark and at least 10° of calibration for verifying ignition timing (spark advance or lead). The harmonic damper or flywheel are the components to which the T.D.C. mark is usually affixed. However, racers usually replace these when rebuilding their engines the T.D.C. reference, unfortunately, is lost. Semi-experienced racers often bring their engines to us for dynamometer testing. It becomes immediately apparent to us that he has been guessing in the dark, without a T.D.C. mark, he has no guide to his spark or valve timing. Without offending this "expert" we calibrated his engine, and trust that he will go forth never to be a "donkey" again. How do you determine T.D.C.? This is explained, along with other Top Tuner's tips in our famous Valve Timing book offered in this ad.

COMMON SENSE BEARING CLEARANCES: How much, if any, extra bearing clearances does a racing engine require over its stock engine counterpart? The first step should be to consult the factory shop manual for their recommended clearances. After all, they built your engine, and their opinion must be respected. However, in a racing engine, where RPM is considerably higher and loads are greater, con rod and main bearing clearances must be given special consideration. It is most important that the con rod "big ends" and crankshaft journals be geometrically round and free of taper. Rods and pistons must be in precise alignment. Some racing engine "experts" increase clearances as much as twice of that recommended. This may work successfully only because it counteracts other misalignment problems. When alignment is correct, extreme clearances are not required. (A basic rule-of-thumb is .001 clearance per inch of journal diameter.) After the existing clearances have been determined, you can then have the crankshaft turned to the proper size, and the rods re-sized if necessary. New rod nuts and bolts should be installed after a magnaflux check for defects.

PARASITIC DRAG IN RACING ENGINES: Today's high performance engines have been proven by dynamometer testing to be 90% mechanically efficient. Therefore, the typical 400 hp engine would have a total frictional drag of 40 hp. By far the greatest contributing factor of this power loss is piston friction, which amounts to a 24 hp loss. The next cause of parasitis drag is unavoidable pumping loss which contributes 10 hp to frictional drag. Finally, and least important, is friction caused by all bearings (crankshaft, con rod, camshaft, etc.), which amounts to a loss of 6 hp. The greater part of this parasitic drag can be attributed

to the crankshaft and con rod bearings as greater loads and higher RPM are imposed upon these components. Today's advanced design camshaft, rotation at only half the speed of the crankshaft, which lift the spring-loaded cam followers individually, requires less than 3 hp to drive. A compressed spring stores potential energy. A basic law of physics is: when power is put in, it is always returned. This stored potential energy helps drive the camshaft. The plain camshaft bearings in today's high-speed engine carry greater loads, without failure, than springs and hi-lift cams can impose upon them. Next month: "Why plain bearings are used in the Dual Overhead Camshaft Racing engines."

WHY PLAIN BEARINGS ARE USED IN DUAL OVERHEAD CAMSHAFT ENGINES: The famous Meyer-Drake D.O.H.C. Offenhauser is probably the most thoroughly race-proven engine in the world today. It has always employed five plain-type bearings on its camshafts for maximum reliability and trouble-free performance. The most recently introduced modern racing engine is the four-cam Ford V-8. Their engineers strived to develop the most powerful and efficient engine possible. This fabulous engine uses plain bearings on all four cam shafts. Recently, another cam manufacturer claimed in their advertising that a gain of up to 40 hp may be had by changing to needle-roller type camshaft bearings. Isn't it logical that even if just a few hp could be positively gained by using this type of bearing, that automotive engineers would have incorporated it into modern D.O.H.C. power plants? There is a popular misconception among many hot rodders that there is metal-to-metal contact in plain-type bearings. This is not true. Actually there is a space (known as bearing clearance) all around the cam bearing journal. This space provides a reservoir with a film of oil under pressure between these metal surfaces. Therefore, the cam bearing journal literally glides on thousands of tiny round molecules of oil to provide a cushion capable of supporting extremely high loads.

HOW DO I SELECT A CAM FOR MY CAR: This is a question asked by many hot rodders. To start, first learn the complete engine specifications, such as: year, make and cubic inches of engine, year of cylinder heads, type of rocker arms and their ratio, compression ratio and carburetion. It is also important to consider the type of chassis, transmission and ratio of differential. Is idling speed important to you? In what engine RPM range would you like to run? Only after learning these basic facts about your engine and chassis it is then possible to determine which racing cam will work best in your engine. Generally a 280° cam with .430 to .450 lift provides the best-all-around performance in the dual purpose car with standard gear ratios and standard transmission. Idling will be a bit faster than stock with a slight lope. For best results, a dual exhaust system should be employed. Also the engine should be equipped with at least a single four-barrel carburetor. Since the 280° racing cam reduces the vacuum in the intake manifold at idle and up to 2,000 RPM, it is recommended that the stock ignition be either replaced or reworked by removing the vacuum advance and replacing it with a full centrifugal advance system. Next month: "Fine tuning your engine."

129

This is an index of Isky's various Top Tuner's Tips articles published over time, most available free to his customers, or for no more than a dollar or so to cover postage and mailing. Lots of tech information for not much money. (Photo Courtesy Ed Iskenderian)

This amusing series of four full-page cartoons deals with the issues of improving fuel economy while maintaining performance during the "gas crunch" of the early 1970s. Isky called its economy performance camshafts "Mile-a-More." Of course, Isky's "go-to" cartoonist and illustrator Pete Millar created these characters and cartoons. (Photos Courtesy Ed Iskenderian)

This 2016 ad illustrates some of Isky's current "roller" valvetrain products, including a few of the slightly whimsical product line names. Creative naming is something Isky has always practiced. (Photo Courtesy Ed Iskenderian)

Among artist Millar's many great illustrations and cartoon characters for Isky Racing Cams ads and creative materials, none has stuck better or means more than his rendering of the famous "Camfather." Ed will happily give you one of the stickers (left) but only he wears one of the patches (right) on his shirt. The only slightly caricatured likeness is amazing, right down to Isky's long-gone full head of dark hair to his trademark stogie, plus the Godfather-like black suit and requisite camshaft. (Photo Courtesy Ed Iskenderian)

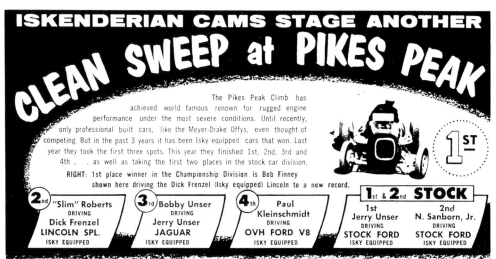

Isky never met a race win he didn't like. This is his ad in Hot Rod *from October 1957, trumpeting a variety of class wins at the Pikes Peak Hillclimb. At the time, Pikes Peak wasn't particularly well known to the public as a popular speed and performance contest, but car builders and big name drivers paid great attention to it and had major feathers in their caps for winning there. Two of the class wins mentioned in this ad involved two of the famous Unser brothers (Jerry and three-time winner Bobby). (Photo Courtesy Ed Iskenderian)*

Ed always believed that his advertisements, in addition to being promotional tools, needed to offer the reader some educational or consumer benefit, hence this full-pager dedicated to camshaft shopping and selection. Note the blurb just above the "write-in" label box at the lower right, advertising Isky Racing Cam T-shirts (sizes small to extra-large only; no XXL back then) for just a dollar. (Photo Courtesy Ed Iskenderian)

Albert Einstein and Ed Iskenderian don't look much alike or really have much in common, but the idea of this ad is to compare Einstein's discovery of the fourth dimension to Isky's innovative "5th cycle" cam design. You have to give credit to Isky and his creative team for decades of creatively named camshaft designs, such as this one: the "5 Cycle Hyperbolic Crossflow 7000," a mouthful of impressive sounding words, if nothing else. (Photo Courtesy Ed Iskenderian)

SPEAKING ABOUT MOTOR MUSIC

ISKENDERIAN RACING CAMS and STRADIVARIUS VIOLINS HAVE A LOT IN COMMON

Antonio Stradivari was a craftsman without peer. For over 200 years no violin maker has ever equalled the remarkable resonance, rich tonal qualities and extraordinary sensitivity of his products. Concert violinists call this the 'Strad response', and all agree — no matter how well they played before — a Strad adds immeasurably to their performance.

Outstanding product mastery, such as this, is not accidental. It calls for an inherent skill plus a ceaseless devotion and dedication to improvement. Throughout the years countless Copy Artists have spuriously labeled their 'fake' violins to capitalize and profit on the Strad reputation. However, the only ones they were able to victimize were the amateurs and bargain hunters — — To the experts these 'facsimilies' are self-betraying as they never match the characteristics of a genuine Strad.

Producing racing camshafts is a far cry from violins, but the same analogy applies. For the past decade Iskenderian has concentrated on a dedicated program of product improvement. While others have been content to merely copy and reap their profits with little or no effort towards research. Isky has constantly maintained a never-ending experimental program of designing and testing. The many innovations introduced by Iskenderian is the history of camshaft development itself and are synonymous with Isky success on the road, on the track, and on the water. Top Tuners and expert engine builders are all familiar with the well known 'Isky response' and all agree that an Isky installation added to their performance. Here, too, the Copy experts have been busy capitalizing on Isky reputation, flooding the market with their facsimilies. They, too, have found their facsimilies self-betraying as they nowhere near match the performance of a genuine Isky.

NOTE: There have been many cases of cam installation switches, some of top name cars, and all familiar to drag racing spectators. Installing an Isky setup has added better than 12 mph to these cars, while changing over from an Isky to another make has made also-rans out of former top cars.

ISKY ROLLER CAM ENGINEERING AMAZES AUTOMOTIVE EXPERTS AT BONNEVILLE

'Sir' Mickey Thompson's Challenger provided one of the biggest automotive engineering achievements of 1959. For here was a 'working', American hot rodder who had the audacity to challenge the records of England's wealthy, 'gentleman' driver, John Cobb, with what must be classified as a home-made machine. The racing world was electrified when he actually broke 16 out of 20 of Cobb's records (Subject to FIA, Paris, France, approval), and under adverse racing strip conditions as well. American hotrod prestige rose to an all time high and gained international respect and admiration as a direct result of 'Sir' Mickey's feats at Bonneville.

'Sir' Mickey widely acclaimed the help of Ed Iskenderian in building his engine and the installed Isky Roller Cams & Kits which gave a flawless performance of all-out power. In fact he actually had to detune his engine for safety purposes because it put out more power than he could use.

Isky Roller Cam & Kit ability to provide outstanding performance is not confined only to all-out competition engines. Witness this case history of an Isky Roller cam installed in a car used for both road and track: Writes Andrew W. Rudolph of Castle Rock, Colo. — . . . . had the misfortune to loose all my oil and as a result the engine seized completely. However, after careful checking of cam we determined it was free of any appreciable wear, this after more than 17,000 miles of hard driving both on and off the track, and an otherwise complete engine failure.'

ISKY PATENTED ROLLER CAM ULTRA-REV KIT

The latest in Isky's long parade of 'firsts'. These kits have been designed to extract even greater power gains and provide more engine efficiency than ever before obtained. Extends engine range over 10,000 rmp without valve float. As with all other Isky innovations, exclusive because of restricted patents, attempts have been made to belittle the effectiveness of these kits. But you can't belittle success . . . and that's what they have proven — in a BIG WAY. Ultra Rev kits are now supplied FREE with all Isky Chev Roller Cams & Kits.

Soon available for other models.

ISKY ENGINEERED CAMS & KITS ARE A STANDOUT IN EVERY CLASS

HI REV CAMS & KITS FOR COMBINATION ROAD & TRACK: These sensational performers, ground on special cast billets, give you by far the most value for your investment. There are plenty of inexpensive grinds around for youngsters toying with their first engine, but for those who want to taste the real thrill of power under the hood there is no substitute for an Isky installation. The little extra investment is returned a hundred fold, both from the standpoint of performance and wear.

FOREIGN CAR ENTHUSIASTS NOTE: Iskenderian is the only cam grinder engaged in full time development of racing grinds for foreign cars. Write direct to our Technical Assistance Dept. for full details . . . or send for new catalog (see below).

SCOOP... 'SWAMP RATS' TAKE HOME THE 'BAIT'!

For the past several months Don Garlits and Art Malone have been heckled, slandered and ridiculed by West Coasters and others who minimized their many victories and records, and even the appearance of their car. He was lured west to the big Riverside Nov. 20 meet by some attractive bait (money), with the idea of polishing him off — but good. Don and Art crossed them all up by eliminating the cream of the west coast — plus other big names, right in their own backyard. His recorded times: 181.45 mph, 8.51 ET. (Full details next issue).

NOW! FORCED INDUCTION KITS FOR CHEV V8's

First time available. Proved a terrific performance booster in repeated dynamometer and field tests. Features a specially developed Edelbrock blower manifold, a 6-71 GMC blower, and an Isky Gilmer belt drive Kit with a built-in water pump. Write for information and prices.

SEND FOR GIANT ISKY CATALOG

The most concise and elaborate cam catalog ever produced. Specifically details and gives full information on all types of grinds for every type engine, plus many valuable tips and useful information...... Only 25c

ED ISKENDERIAN
607 North Inglewood Avenue, Dept. H3
Inglewood, California   ORegon 8-7791

"Proven The World's Best"

'KNOW YOUR SPARK LEAD'

This is only one of the many valuable top tuners tips to be fully discussed and explained in Isky's tremendous popular book. A must for every veteran engine builder as well as the beginner. Explodes many myths and is the most completely authenticated treatise ever written.

VALVE TIMING

VALVE TIMING FOR MAXIMUM OUTPUT
$1.00 POSTPAID

Hmm . . . comparing a camshaft to a Stradivarius violin is a bit of a stretch in anyone's book, but not Isky's. The engine-music implication is fun and aims to make the connection between items of great design and the highest-production values. Although Ed loves music, he doesn't own a Strad or play the violin. This ad is from March 1960. (Photo Courtesy Ed Iskenderian)

185.566 MPH NEW WORLD RECORD ¼ Mile

GARLITS EXPLODES TO NEW MARK AT BROOKSVILLE, FLA.

They say that records are made only to be broken, and **Don Garlits**, the Tampa Terror, is such a staunch believer in this adage that racing officials now enter his records in pencil — for easy erasure. Following his big triumph in the final run of the U.S. Fuel-Gas Championships at Lodi, Calif., Don predicted he might hit 190 mph before too long. Many scoffed and dismissed this as 'headline-seeking' talk; but after this latest record shattering run a lot of opinions have been revised. Garlits attributes much of his new found power to the **new, sensational Isky, Gilmer beltdriven Forced Induction Kit** and, of course, the always dependable power of the **Isky 5 Cycle Cam and Engineered Kit**.

THE RECORD THAT WAS NEVER REPORTED — THE LODI MISCUE

A new world record was actually established at Lodi during the 2nd run of the U.S. Fuel-Gas meet . . . but was never released. Here are details. After trying several fuel combinations Garlits settled on a 50% mixture and then made one of his monumental runs. Unbelieving officials looked twice and gasped . . and then asked for an impartial observer. Before he got there, however, they asked the operator at the Crondex clocks to push the 'SET' button. Instead he mistakenly pushed the 'RESET' button. According to Strip Manager, Bob Cress, 3 officials witnessed the time but because of the unfortunate mistake realized that any official sanction might be construed as 'fixed'. Discreet confidence, therefore, was maintained until Garlits vindicated a future announcement of this phenomenal run.

GOOD NEWS FOR DRAGSTERS WITH RESTRICTED BUDGETS

Even though your working capital is stretched rather thin you'll soon know what it's like to hit the magic 180 mph class. Isky Engineers are completing final tests on grinds for the economical early, 331 cu. in. Chryslers ('51-'54), supercharged. These 'salvage-type' engines that can be picked up for a song indicate that they're capable of better than 180 mph on fuel and 160 mph on gas. Our recent poll on Formula, U.S.A. indicated opinion evenly divided on size limitations of engines. However, based on readers' comments we predict that strip operators will eventually organize separate classes for the smaller engines.

THE ISKY 5 CYCLE PARADE OF VICTORIES AND RECORDS CONTINUES TO MOUNT
TONY WATERS' ROADSTER DERAILS SUPER RAIL JOBS

Top dragsters are fervently wishing the team of **Tony Waters** and **Jim Segrue** had chosen any sport but drag racing as they continue to deflate their pride with amazing runs in their roadster-bodied, small engine De Soto. A select group of top names was invited to compete at the Henderson strip in Las Vegas, and when the final fumes had settled Waters once again had taken **Top Eliminator** honors, beating everything in sight, including the 180 mph dragster. He also took **Top Time** with a sensational 176 mph run. His Isky 5 Cycle powered car has been appropriately named the 'Giant Killer'.

FLASH: NEW WORLD RECORD FOR DRAG BOATS

John Simas of Fresno, Calif., treated a huge turnout at the Hart Park Course to a sensational exhibit of marine power as he piloted his aptly named 'White Mist' to 4 successive runs over the existing world record for the ¼ mile. Powered by a 392 cu. in. Chrysler (Supercharged and equipped with an **Isky 5 Cycle Blower Cam and Kit**) his boat actually made the 1st run of 101.91 mph on straight alcohol, although the former record had been set on a nitro-methane mixture. His fastest time for which recognition has been filed was 110.56 mph. Boat is co-owned by **Jack Davidson (Sanger Hull Co.).** Engine was built by Hashim Automotive of Bakersfield, Calif.

DRAG STRIPS and RACE TRACKS ARE BUT PROVING GROUNDS TO ESTABLISH THE FACT THAT . . . .

YOU GET MORE DOLLAR VALUE FROM ISKENDERIAN CAMS AND KITS

It's quite natural that the fastest engines receive the headlines, but one fact is always obvious. The manufacturer that has the know-how to produce winning combinations in the top classes must use this same knowledge to produce superior products in ALL classes. Iskenderian Cams not only produce exceptional power, but they're engineered for long life and trouble free performance — the most ECONOMICAL COMBINATION OF ALL.

ONLY ISKENDERIAN
GIVES YOU PROTECTION THREE WAYS —
BEFORE YOU BUY! WHEN YOU BUY! AFTER YOU BUY!

LOOK! See CHAMPS IN ACTION .. on 16MM COLOR FILM

Iskenderian has done it again! In order to bring all the thrills, action, and sound of a big drag meet to the thousands of enthusiasts who have no opportunity to view such an event, we commissioned a professional crew to film and record the highlights of the recent U.S. FUEL-GAS twin meets. Copies are now being processed and will be available for lease to clubs, schools, etc. Write **immediately** for details and reservations.

ISKY ROLLER CAMS and ENGINEERED KITS

ISKY 5 CYCLE CAMS and ENGINEERED KITS

ISKY HI-REV CAMS and ENGINEERED KITS

VALVE TIMING FOR MAXIMUM OUTPUT
New 1959 spring edition now available. A must for every top tuner and newcomer to fully understand valve gear action. **ONLY $1.00.**

NEW 1959 CATALOG
Soon off the press. New giant size with complete information on Rollers, Hi-Rev, 5 Cycle, Foreign and Sports Cars, Micro-Midgets, Go-Karts, Motorcycles, Marine, etc.
25c per copy (postpaid)

ED ISKENDERIAN
607 North Inglewood Avenue, Dept. H, Inglewood, California · ORegon 8-7791

Ed wisely continued to hammer home his sponsorship of Don Garlits, a worthwhile pursuit; Garlits won almost everywhere he went and went on to become one of drag racing's winningest and most popular drivers. This ad, from July 1957, also went on to mention Isky Racing Cams' sponsorship of Sanger Boats' White Mist drag boats. (Photo Courtesy Ed Iskenderian)

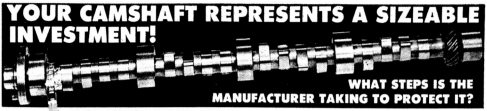

This June 1959 ad features a variety of cars and themes. However, the most significant among them is in the middle of the page and celebrates Lee Petty's big win at the Daytona 500. The engine in his 1959 Olds was a new design that year, and Petty trusted only Iskenderian to design and grind up a winning camshaft. Polesitter Cotton Owns also ran an Isky cam. (Photo Courtesy Ed Iskenderian)

This January 1959 full-pager covered not only the latest low ETs and future appearance schedule of Isky poster child Garlits, but also the dominating race-winning performance of Lance Reventlow's all-American-built Scarab road racers. These handsome, Ferrari-esque road racers were powered by highly tuned, multi-carb small-block Chevy V-8s, something Isky knew a thing or two about. It also didn't hurt that the Isky's Inglewood, California, facility was only a few miles away from Scarab's Culver City–area race shop. (Photo Courtesy Ed Iskenderian)

Seldom did Isky stop beating the drum for his 5-Cycle Cam philosophy, here noting a variety of recent race records and wins earned by 5-Cycle–equipped cars. He also never missed slipping a cute cartoon into one of his ads; the little illustration at the top features a new Chevrolet Fleetside truck with a bedload of recent NHRA drag racing trophies. (Photo Courtesy Ed Iskenderian)

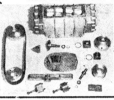

Besides consistently underscoring Isky Racing Cams sponsorship of and relationship with Don Garlits, another theme worthy of a constant reminder was Isky's role as sponsor and camshaft provider for Mickey Thompson's legendary Challenger I Bonneville record holder. The main message of this ad from Hot Rod in October 1959 appears to be the notion of buying not just a camshaft, but a cam and kit of coordinated valvetrain components. Also, in the center of the right column is mention and a photo of Isky's supercharger kits; Isky didn't produce the GMC blowers but did design and engineer the blower drive systems. (Photo Courtesy Ed Iskenderian)

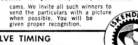
In this November 1958 Hot Rod ad, Isky makes the connection between his 5-cycle cam profile design and the achievement of ultimate volumetric efficiency, the notion of filling the cylinder fully with atomized fuel and air to get the maximum combustion out of each piston cycle. It's difficult to imagine how something could be more than 100 percent; perhaps the high compression and supercharging of Garlits' dragster made up the additional 10 percent to get to 110. A bit of hyperbole? Perhaps, but you can't argue with the wins, record times, and results. (Photo Courtesy Ed Iskenderian)

"TV" Tommy Ivo was much more than a hot rodder or actor who drag raced just for fun and for the equivalent of Twitter hits. Ivo was a talented quarter-mile pilot with many notable race wins to his credit. Ivo often ran Isky cams. This unsupercharged gasser rail was lightning fast, running the quarter in less than 9 seconds; that's crazy fast for a naturally aspirated Buick. (Photo Courtesy Ed Iskenderian)

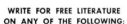

If something is worth saying once, it's worth saying again. And again and again. So it was with Iskenderian's 5-cycle camshaft and the success that Don Garlits enjoyed with it (before he became Big Daddy). This ad also offers an information box explaining the theories behind the mythical fifth combustion cycle. Science or hokum? Doesn't matter, it obviously worked. From Hot Rod *in February 1962. (Photo Courtesy Ed Iskenderian)*

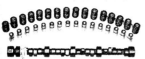

Along with the well-deserved mention of big-name racing efforts by drivers such as Mickey Thompson and Don Garlits, Isky's ads often featured "little guy" racers and smaller private or backyard efforts. One example of this was featured in this April 1964 ad that talks about the J & J Headers 1950 Chevy four-door sedan. This 3,700-pound-plus, 283 Chevy-equipped machine ran in the D/Gas category, putting down consistent mid-13-second quarter-mile times with none other than Isky employee Bones Balough at the wheel. (Photo Courtesy Ed Iskenderian)

INDEX